Duchess

An Intimate Portrait of Sarah, Duchess of York

ANDREW MORTON

CB

CONTEMPORARY
BOOKS

CHICAGO · NEW YORK

Library of Congress Cataloging-in-Publication Data

Morton, Andrew, 1953–
    Duchess : an intimate portrait of Sarah, Duchess of York /
Andrew Morton.
       p.   cm.
    Includes index.
    ISBN 0-8092-4438-1 : $16.95
    1. York, Sarah Mountbatten-Windsor, Duchess of, 1959–
    2. Great Britain—Nobility—Biography.   I. Title.
DA591.A45Y676   1989
941.085′092′4—dc19
[B]   88-34260
                                                CIP

First published in Great Britain by
Michael O'Mara Books Limited

Published by Contemporary Books, Inc.
180 North Michigan Avenue, Chicago, Illinois 60601
Manufactured in the United States of America
Library of Congress Catalog Card Number: 88-34260
International Standard Book Number: 0-8092-4438-1

Published simultaneously in Canada by Beaverbooks, Ltd.
195 Allstate Parkway, Valleywood Business Park
Markham, Ontario L3R 4T8 Canada

Contents

Acknowledgments

This is the first biography of HRH the Duchess of York. There will be others on this young woman who, I believe, will establish the tone and style of the House of Windsor for the next century—if the royal family is to survive at all.

In drawing this initial portrait of the Duchess I am indebted to the help and guidance of Lady Annaly, Major Bill Anderson, Sally Armstrong, Beverley Bailey, Peter Cunard, William Drummond, Alan Hamilton, Larry Kent, John Latimer, Ken Lennox, Philippa MacKinnon, Tristan Millington-Drake, Michael Noakes, Gareth Pyne-James, Tim Satchell, Ingrid Seward, David Thompson, Clem Tousignant, Sarah Worsley and the Duchess's other friends and acquaintances who have preferred to remain in the background.

I am specially indebted to Major Ronald and Mrs. Susan Ferguson, who clarified many details of the Duchess's early life.

Finally my thanks to my wife, Lynne, for her support and the enthusiasm of Michael and Lesley O'Mara and their staff.

1
The Fergie Factor

S he enjoys roast beef, Elton John, and downhill skiing—
but not necessarily in that order. She collects English
architectural drawings, eighteenth-century watercolors,
and silly cartoons. She loathes snakes, snobs, and psychol-
ogy. She has the ear of the Queen, an unerring eye for detail,
and the measure of her *bête noire*, Koo Stark.

She loves fresh raspberries, champagne, and the Princess
of Wales's fizzy sense of fun. She cooks as well as she plays
the piano—"Me play the piano, you must be joking," she
says. She is determinedly middlebrow yet with one eye scan-
ning the horizon for the offbeat, the eccentric. She is knowl-
edgeable about medieval Bibles, and admires antique books
but reads John Le Carré and Len Deighton for pleasure. She
affects a certain aesthetic philistinism yet can speak with
authority about Pissarro, Pugin, and paper making. She
listens to Capital Radio, loves weepie black and white films,
and adores real men like Clint Eastwood, Paul Newman, and
"Superman" Christopher Reeve.

Her Royal Highness the Duchess of York. Prince Andrew

calls her "darling," the royal family speak of her as "Sarah York," her father calls her "G.B.," her friends call her "ma'am" in public, Sarah in private, and the rest of the world knows her as "Fergie." But Sarah Margaret Ferguson is no longer a commoner even though she has the common touch. "My name is not Sarah," she firmly tells over-familiar photographers. By the time the Duchess had been in the public eye for a mere thousand days, she had indelibly stamped her inimitable style on the royal family, a tone that can be defined as "dignified informality." "She has packed more into the last two years than most people do in a lifetime," says her stepmother, Susan Ferguson, with more than a touch of pride. She has taken elevation to the House of Windsor in her bustling stride, relishing the pomp, the circumstance, the tradition.

Motherhood has not dominated her crowded life, where every day is spent trying to pour a quart into a pint pot. Her partnership with Andrew has brought unquestionable happiness, a love she wants to share with the world. "She is total sunshine," says Bill Drummond, a former employer and friend. "With that heavenly halo of Titian hair she is a photographer's dream."

. She has steady green-gray eyes that switch from the impish to the imperious, a firm jaw, a hugely mobile face, and strong white teeth, which in conjunction with Andrew's hearty laugh give the impression of two Steinway grand pianos playing in tandem. The Duchess is from sturdy yeoman stock and her circle of friends—and hence future courtiers—is tilled from that same soil: lesser aristocrats with a bent for business, upper-class women with the wit and will to start their own companies and who are practical, ambitious, and aware. The pretty, the pouting, and the passive do not find fertile ground in her affections. She is an example and exponent of the "Can Do" philosophy, a "let's get on with it" attitude that finds an enthusiastic echo in the New World. They see in the Duchess an embodiment of the New Woman of the late twentieth century. She is energetic, outgoing, pragmatic, and believes that marriage is an active and equal partnership and that motherhood should not stifle a flourishing career. While the Duchess supports her husband, she equally demands care and consideration in return. Hence she learned to fly helicopters and small aircraft not only to show her love for him but also to fulfill herself. "She is a woman who knows herself, is at peace with herself, and derives a great deal of strength through that," observed David Thompson, the wilderness expert who accompanied the Duchess during her canoeing adventure through Canada's sub-Arctic in 1987. Besides being instrumental in saving her life, David observed a young woman entirely at ease with her husband and very much in love.

It is not a sentiment one could ascribe to every royal marriage. The Yorks have a robust, giggly, and physical relationship, often behaving like a pair of playful Labradors. After every statement Andrew has the habit of saying, "Isn't that right darling" in the way of all young couples. She teases him mercilessly, her streetwise savvy more than a match for his pedestrian, patrician style. Andrew in a pedantic mood sets her eyes revolving like lemons in a fruit machine to exaggerate her boredom.

She is a natural and informal character who bridles at the pompous and prurient. It is a quality which the royal portrait artist, Michael Noakes, drew out in his study of the Duchess. He had her pose in a casual shirt, her red hair tumbling over the sweater draped over her shoulders. "She is a very bubbly girl," he says. "The Duchess exudes a kind of relaxed dignity which I tried to capture." Mr. Noakes, who has painted most of the royal family, was charmed and surprised to receive a call from her before one sitting at his St. John's Wood house. "Is that Michael or Ben?" (his novelist son) she said. "Sorry I'm late, I'm on my way." "Normally they leave that sort of thing to ladies-in-waiting or other members of staff," explained Mr. Noakes. Her open friendliness, that endearing bounding Labrador quality, does not command universal acclaim. "She devalues the currency," was Princess Michael of Kent's tart verdict. "All that winking at the wedding."

Staff at Buckingham Palace, a sniffy lot at the best of

times, are not enamored. They still remember with affection Prince Andrew's former love, the actress Koo Stark. He brought her to the kitchens to meet the servants. Koo, poised, cool, self-contained, sat and drank coffee and nibbled croissants. "She was the one for him," recalls one senior member of staff. "Shame they were stopped from marrying."

As a breed, servants tend to be conservative and rather stuffier than their principals. As yet they cannot cope with a breezy Duchess, so positive in public but hesitant in private, an indecision that frequently boils over into bossiness.

Her first dresser, Caroline Terry, left after ten months complaining that the Duchess could not make up her mind about what to wear. She would prepare four or five outfits to wear in anticipation, only to be confronted by a last minute change of heart. She is now filling shelves in a London supermarket.

That thread of insecurity which runs through the Duchess's character is normally masked by her hearty high spirits. "She wants to be loved, wants to be liked," say her friends. The Duchess comes from an unsettled home—her parents, Major Ronald and Susie Ferguson, were divorced when she was an impressionable teenager. Her previous romantic relationships were characterized as much by tears and sad goodbyes as laughter and stability.

Indeed, it is a tribute to her indomitable will and firmness of character that a life of aimless hedonism has been transformed to enable her to play a crucial role within the royal family. Just three years ago she was in the depths of despair, her life a mess, her romance with motor racing executive Paddy McNally in a downward spiral, her friends and family wringing their hands about her future. The radical change in her circumstances has allowed her true nature to come shining through. It is little wonder then that she chose Jennifer Rush's "The Power of Love" as the television anthem on the eve of her wedding day, or that her family motto is *Ex adversis felicitas crescit*—"Out of adversity happiness grows"!

Since her marriage she has followed her father's advice to "be yourself, be natural." Of course there is more poise, style, and sophistication, but the Duchess is still the same old Fergie. It is one of the most refreshing aspects of her new royal life. Ingrid Seward, editor of *Majesty* magazine and a friend from her bachelor days, says: "She has not changed, and I am really impressed by her remaining so unspoilt."

This is a constant refrain of friends and family. Bill Drummond is endlessly impressed by her thoughtfulness: "Even now she still finds time to write to my daughters at school. Just little notes saying, 'How are you getting on? or Hope you are working hard.' One would have accepted it if in her new exalted situation she did not have the time. But she keeps something going. A very generous woman."

She is determined to stay in touch with the friends and habits from her bachelor days. This preserves her independence and keeps her feet on the ground, living as she does in a rarified atmosphere of gentility and genuflection.

Naturally she has regrets. When she lunches with girlfriends she becomes wistful as they talk gaily of weekend trips, of plans for tennis, and barbecues—"I wish I could do these things but I can't anymore," she moans. For now she is surrounded by private secretaries, ladies-in-waiting, equerries, and Scotland Yard bodyguards who dog her footsteps. On one occasion when she tried a solo escape bid from Buckingham Palace she was spotted by a vigilant uniformed policeman who urgently radioed her bodyguard. He followed hotfoot in pursuit and in breathless admonition told her: "I wish you wouldn't do that, ma'am."

It was the anticipated loss of the spontaneity of her carefree bachelor life that prompted her to refuse Andrew when he first broached the question of marriage during a New Year's stay at Sandringham. Here the similarities with the Queen Mother, with whom she is often compared, become uncanny. Both have an unerring instinct for the cameras, and the Queen Mother also rejected the marriage proposal of George V's second son because she did not want to involve herself with the showy, self-conscious but ultimately sterile life at Court. When she finally accepted Bertie's hand she proved herself, during the abdication crisis and the Second

World War, to be the pivot around which the House of Windsor rose or fell. A similar responsibility rests on the freckled shoulders of the Duchess of York, as the royal family faces the challenges of the twenty-first century. Though it does not have a crisis of the monumental proportions of the abdication to surmount, the royal family is at a critical watershed, a turning point where its traditional veiled mystique is being stripped bare by the twin pressures of commercialization and television. It is a striptease act in which some members of the family have conspired, much to the dismay of others. As one member commented, "I believe the royal family is doomed if it continues down this path. It is the price you pay for courting publicity. It will become too cheap and nobody will want it. The royal family exist by their scarcity value. At the moment it is a firework. Spectacular for a short while and then burns itself out."

The dilemma facing the royal family of remaining approachable but aloof cuts to the very core of its *raison d'être*. During the reign of Queen Elizabeth II the royal family has developed two principal functions—to represent the State as living symbols of the country and to support worthy causes. However, it is their charitable function that is undercutting their primary role. As one member of the family put it: "In trying to help charities, they are helping to destroy themselves. Great mistakes have been made for the best possible motives."

The problem has been that during the 1980s we have seen the royal family become far more media conscious in order to raise money for their particular causes. So the Prince and Princess of Wales allowed ITN television cameras to follow them at work and play for a year. The result was two charming documentaries which raised millions of pounds for charity. Nevertheless, the royal couple were franchising themselves, renting out their royalty, to help charity. Then followed Prince Edward's notorious Royal Knockout Tournament which included the Duke and Duchess of York, and the Princess Royal, and raised £1 million for four charities. But television, by its very nature, is a remorseless medium. The shading of the difference between what we think of as royalty and showbiz has now become negligible.

The Rent-a-Royal syndrome is illustrated in a joke about the Prince and Princess of Wales that was current in West Palm Beach when they were guests of honor at a dinner which had various rates of admission depending on proximity to the royal couple. The story went like this:

A wealthy Texan arrived at West Palm Beach and asked the charity organizer what he would get for $15,000.

"For that," said the organizer, "you get in to the dinner."

"What do I get for $50,000?" drawled the Texan.

"Well, you get to shake hands with the Princess of Wales."

"OK, what do I get for $100,000?"

"You get your picture taken with the Princess."

"How about for $200,000?"

"You get to speak to the Princess at dinner."

"How about for $400,000?"

"You get to sit next to the Princess at dinner."

"OK," said the Texan, "I'll go for broke. What do I get for $1 million?"

"You get to dance with Joan Collins."

It is this devaluing of the royal family—a process that has gathered pace during the 1980s—that is the most insidious and difficult problem to resolve.

Against this background the Duchess has made her mistakes. At the Royal Knockout Tournament her rambunctious manner, where she lost her voice shouting for her team and started an undignified food fight with her husband, did not accord with the public's perception of royal behavior. Similarly, her antics at Royal Ascot with the Princess of Wales, where they prodded the bottom of their friend, Lulu Blacker, with their brollies and then proceeded to wolf whistle at Princess Michael of Kent, did her image little good.

Her appearance on various television and radio shows to promote a book about the Houses of Parliament which she had commissioned for her Geneva-based publishing company encapsulated the challenge that the Duchess presents to the royal family. As a working Duchess—itself almost a contradiction in terms—she used her royal position to make money not for charity, but for her own company. Royalty and commerce make unhappy bedfellows. "A mistake, it is wrong to use the name of the royal family to sell a commercial book," said one member of the family.

The Duchess cheerfully accepts that she will make blunders. "I am going to make some mistakes and will get things wrong, and you might just as well accept it," she has told her husband. Yet it is vital for the future of the royal family that she does get things right. By the year 2000, only twelve short years away, she and the Princess of Wales will be the most influential members of the royal family. Over the next couple of decades we will witness the gradual diminishing of the royal family "Firm" as the scaffolding that surrounds the House of Windsor is gradually dismantled. The Queen, the Duke of Edinburgh, the Queen Mother, Princess Margaret, the Kents, and the Ogilvies will either be in semiretirement or the victims of the passage of time. There are few, if any, of the younger royal generation willing to shore up the edifice. The burden will be left for the Waleses, the Yorks, and the Princess Royal to carry. Much of the somber weight of continuity will rest on the royal ladies. Traditionally, the House of Windsor has been a matriarchal family. During the twenty-first century petticoat power will devolve upon two commoners, the Princess of Wales and the Duchess of York. A similar alliance existed in the eighteenth century between Queen Anne and the domineering Sarah, Duchess of Marlborough. Their uneasy relationship of intrigue and conspiracy ended in harsh and bitter words uttered in the Queen's closet at Kensington Palace.

By contrast, the Princess of Wales and the Duchess of York characterize their friendship as "wonderful." At Court the Princess is senior and the Duchess accepts this fact of royal protocol. In personal relations it is the Duchess who is the dominant partner. The fact that the Princess of Wales has a friend at the Palace has come as something of a relief to the royal family. Sarah is seen as a stayer, Diana as a bolter. It is

the Waleses' marriage which has come under continual scrutiny, a fact that has merely added to the existing strains.
Diana's friends, too, worry that she will not stay the course.
As one has said: "If courtiers try and keep her on a tight rein
she may run. With Sarah around she is able to let off steam."

It is the Princess of Wales who leaves Kensington Palace in
her nightie and raincoat and drives off alone into the night to
visit girlfriends who live locally. "She just likes to get away
and try and lead a normal life," says one friend. The Duchess
has been a shoulder to cry on, someone to rely on for the last
eight years as she has coped with two difficult pregnancies
and a marriage that would be hard to characterize as normal.
The Princess and the Duchess are a Mutual Protection
Society, standing firm against the pressures of the family,
the demands of the media, and the shared frustrations of
giving up their independence for title and position. If Diana
is envious of Sarah, it is the jealousy of one who feels she has
missed out on her youth and sees that worldly experience
manifested in a friend.

It is a worldly shrewdness that has brought the Duchess
acceptance within the royal family. "They like her because
she is the one who has tried," explained one friend. She has
cultivated the Queen, seeing her for afternoon tea and dinner
at Buckingham Palace. The talk is of country matters, the
navy, her publishing work, horses, and dogs. Sarah is a
nonstop chatterbox who has never been daunted by the
Queen, who was intensely proud of Sarah's achievement in
canoeing down the Thelon River in Canada in 1987. During
the Queen's visit to that country she enjoyed listening as the
locals told her just how dangerous the trip had been, in
confirmation of her daughter-in-law's own account of her
adventure. "Her Majesty admitted that she was very worried
about her at the time," recalls one Toronto cocktail guest.

The Queen's affection for the Duchess—she is paying an
estimated £1 million to build her royal home—is shared by
other members of the royal family. "A very natural person
with a rare gift for the job," says one member with a touch of
admiration. "It is not easy to come in from outside." She has

gone out of her way to woo the family. She has tried carriage-
and-four driving with Prince Philip, skis alongside Prince
Charles who even comes to Buckingham Palace for his hair-
cutting by her stylist, and has earned the praise of the
Princess Royal, a tough judge of character who was muted in
her assessment of the Princess of Wales. "A very, very nice
girl," she says, "Andrew is very lucky."

Not that it is all one-way traffic. "A Coronation Street
Princess," Princess Michael of Kent said of her after the royal
wedding. Shrewdly the Princess has recognized the reality of
the Duchess's impact on the House of Windsor. "She is
strong and independent. You watch, Fergie will change us
all." However others complain that she spends more time
looking for cameras than concentrating on the job. In the
fashion trade there is some resentment that she uses her
position to drive too hard a bargain. When she asked designer Zandra Rhodes for a discount in return for publicity,
Miss Rhodes replied: "My darling, I don't *need* the publicity." As one friend says: "That's Fergie, she is a naturally
competitive person and will always try and strike a deal no
matter how much she is worth." For while she has been
surrounded by millionaires, money has never been heaven
sent. The allowance from her father, Major Ronald Ferguson,
has never been a royal ransom. She has spent much of her
working life pleasing people in order to clinch deals. "A
natural saleswoman," says one former boss. "An incredible
memory for people's names, their likes and dislikes."

Her business acumen has been readily grafted onto her
growing charity work. While the world has taken notice of
how hard she plays, little has been said of how hard she
works. Numerous charities of which she is the patron or
president speak warmly of the Duchess. "She is very much a
hands-on patron," is one verdict, for she insists that she does
not simply want to be a figurehead. In her work promoting
the Tate Gallery Foundation, for example, she uses her sales
techniques to flatter and impress businessmen at working
lunches. "Before every meeting she wants to know what we
want out of it and how she can help," says one official. "Quite

simply she is jolly good at buttering up important people."

She works from her fourth floor study overlooking the Mall in Buckingham Palace. It is a cozy room, full of family photographs—Andrew in his helicopter gear, her father playing polo. On the conference table are aviation magazines, flight manuals, and her flying helmet—a reminder of her newfound enthusiasm for the skies. There is also a giant teddy snugly hidden in one corner, indicative of her irreverent informality. Her appointment calendar is full and controlled efficiently by her lady-in-waiting, Helen Hughes, a friend from the old days. Visitors are impressed by her brisk friend-liness, her searching questions, her constructive suggestions.

Before the launch of the best-selling book, *A Day for Life*, in aid of the Search 88 cancer charity of which she is patron, the Duchess convened a meeting at the Palace to discuss the press party. She quickly essayed the fine details before finish-ing with the secret of winning the hearts of the media. "Give them champagne, caviar, and canapés and you are sure of good reviews," she said, speaking from experience of the publishing world. Then she paused, realized possible pitfalls, and said: "As we are a charity we had better forget the champagne. Shame."

The Duchess is used to breaking new ground, a royal frontierswoman much admired by the Australians, Ameri-cans, and Canadians. She was the first royal to appear on a record sleeve—it didn't help the single "Hold On," which flopped in the charts—and, the first royal female to hold a private pilot's license and a private helicopter license. More-over, it is remarkable that the house the Duke and Duchess will build several miles from Windsor Castle is the first and only example of royal building during the reign of Queen Elizabeth II. That fact alone says much about the vigor and enthusiasm with which the Duchess of York has entered into her royal life. Unlike Captain Mark Phillips or the Princess of Wales, the Duchess has refused to be smothered by the Windsors. While other "in-laws"—the Phillipses, the Spencers, the Tomasellis, the von Riebnitzes—fade into convenient obscurity, the Ferguson family have grown in

stature and self-assurance. We can already see the beginnings
of a Ferguson dynasty as the Duchess, aware that her first
child could conceivably one day rule the country and Com-
monwealth, stamps her signature on this reign and puts
down a marker for the next.

It is no surprise to find that her father, Major Ronald
Ferguson, whom she sees each week for lunch at Claridge's,
once worked for a public relations company, Neilson McCar-
thy, which helped polish Prince Charles's image during the
turbulent 1960s. His frequent but uncontentious pronounce-
ments on his daughter have helped bypass the Palace and
place her thoughts and feelings in front of the public in a way
that is as discreet as it is effective. The Duchess has also
learned from the mistakes of the Princess of Wales. She has
not been intimidated by the Palace machine or swamped by
protocol. Just as she has knocked the starch out of Prince
Andrew, she has pounded the stuffiness out of the Palace.
She is determined that her family, her friends, and her previous life should not be frozen out simply because she has
joined the world's most influential and famous family.

She insisted on creating her own family coat of arms, to
the surprise of her father, but she stood firm. Her independent attitude is seen in the way she behaves in public and is
highlighted by the home she is having built. Unlike Prince
Charles who often talks about the failings of modern architecture, the Duchess has acted and made a personal statement. The house itself, a low-slung, ranch-style home, is in
the mold of Southfork. In her "Palace Dallas" one half
expects to see J.R., whisky in hand, lurching out of the
stables. "It will be a lot nicer than that," she argues. "When
did you see an architect's drawing resemble the finished
article?" Yet the building itself, mocked as "Tudorbethan," is
indicative of the tone she has set and will continue to set in
the years to come.

For the Duchess of York's style heralds a new age for the
royal family. The last hundred years have seen the Windsors
remorselessly English in their tastes and attitudes. This has
been promoted both to disguise their German origins and to

symbolize national life. So royal holidays have made the inevitable round of Windsor, Sandringham, and Balmoral. Hobbies and sports have been aristocratically and eccentrically English—fishing, hunting, shooting, stamp collecting. Prince Charles is never happier than when he is tramping over the heather on the Queen's Highland estate. The Princess of Wales, for all that she may chafe at the royal bit, is the quintessential English rose, who wears British clothes and patronizes British interior designers. The Waleses deliberately and publicly fly the Union Jack. With the arrival of the Duchess, we see a challenge to this John Bull image. She enjoys Barbados as much as Balmoral, skiing as much as Sandringham. Her first-choice interior designers, Sister Parish and Albert Hadley were American, her dress designer, Yves St. Laurent, is French. Her home eschews the normal Georgian clichés and veers towards the international, the cosmopolitan. In a very public way, the Duchess is the first fully paid-up member of the royal jet set, the first Yuppie Royal.

As the years go by the "Fergie Factor" will become more apparent and her positive, sure, and conservative cosmopolitan style will materially change the nature of the royal family as it stands at a crossroads in its development.

She has been dealt a strong hand, the way she plays it will establish whether the royal family survives or fades away. This is her story. . . .

2
Early Days

*D*uty, *service, and responsibility.* As befitting a military family these have been the watchwords of the Ferguson clan for generations. Well connected, well-to-do, and well regarded, the Fergusons form part of the backbone of the English gentry. Their ancestry is rooted firmly in the land and the Services. It was into this world of solid yeoman stock and values that Ronald Ivor Ferguson was born in 1931, the second son of the then Major Andrew Ferguson and Marian Montagu-Douglas-Scot, granddaughter of the Sixth Duke of Buccleuch. Like his father before him he went to Ludgrove preparatory school then Eton and Sandhurst, where he won a commission to the Life Guards. It was a well-worn route and one to which red-haired Ronald was ideally suited. At school he was not a scholar, preferring the games field to the library. "I'm a physical person, not a mental person," he says. "I would loathe sitting in an office in London as a stockbroker or a barrister. That was never for me."

His elder brother, John Andrew, would have inevitably

followed a similar path but at ten he was tragically struck down with peritonitis, leaving Ronald heir to the family farm at Dummer, Hampshire, and flag bearer of an illustrious Service heritage.

His father rose to become colonel and commanding officer of the Life Guards, commanding the Sovereign's Escort of the Household Cavalry for George V's Silver Jubilee parade. His grandfather, Brigadier-General Algernon Francis Ferguson, had served in the Boer War and commanded a regiment of the Life Guards during the First World War. He was the High Sheriff of Northamptonshire, residing in Polebrook Hall which he inherited from his elder brother, Major Victor Ferguson, who was killed during the Battle of Ashanti in 1896.

The Life Guards connection was started by Major Ferguson's great grandfather, Colonel John Ferguson, who transferred to this élite regiment after serving with the Dragoon Guards in the Crimean war between 1854 and 1856, seeing active duty at Balaclava and Sebastopol.

However, the Ferguson family is of Irish origin. The earliest traceable ancestor is Dr. James Ferguson, a Belfast linen manufacturer, who died in 1784. His son, John, and grandson, Thomas, lived at Greenville, County Down, the latter sailing to England to increase his fortune. He married Emma Benyon of New Grange Hall, Leeds, leaving his eldest son, John, to forge a highly successful military career and his second son, Thomas, to pursue life as a barrister in the law courts.

So, in August 1949, when Ronald Ferguson joined the Life Guards, he was continuing 150 years of honorable service, a tradition displayed in Dummer parish church where the gold embroidered Guards standard is a permanent reminder of the family links with this most fashionable of regiments.

He served for twenty years in Germany, Cyprus, and Aden and, like his father before him, commanded the Sovereign's Escort. On one legendary occasion the Queen had to order him to rein in during a parade. "Back a bit Ronald," she told him. "It's me they have come to see, not you."

Then, as now, he was a stickler for detail and precision. When drummer "Dolly" Gray missed two beats during the Queen's Birthday Parade, Major Ferguson fined him the princely sum of £3.8s6d for "idleness on parade." Before another parade in Edinburgh he spotted that the horses of the Household Cavalry were unsettled by the skirl of the bagpipes. Rather than take a chance, he organized a troop of the Argyll and Sutherland Highlanders to play for the 120 regimental horses so they would get used to the wheezing of the pipes. This organizational ability and attention to detail is a characteristic his daughter Sarah has inherited.

While he rose to the rank of major, it was as a dashing young lieutenant that Ronald Ferguson first caught the eye of an attractive debutante, Susie Mary Wright, the daughter of the Honorable Doreen Wingfield and Fitzherbert Wright, formerly of the 15th/19th Hussars. She had been presented to the Queen at Buckingham Palace when she "came out" in 1955, together with other debutantes who included the Duchess of Rutland and the actress Anna Massey. Like the Fergusons, the Wrights have Irish ancestry, Susie's grandfather was the Irish senator, Eighth Viscount Powerscourt of Enniskerry, County Wicklow. Indeed, through blood and intermarriage the Wright family are connected with most of the illustrious houses of Britain and can trace their English roots back much further than the Fergusons.

The first recorded ancestor was a certain John Wright who lived in Stowmarket, Suffolk until his death in 1559. The family moved to Nottinghamshire where Captain John Wright distinguished himself in the Civil War. Ironically he fought for the Parliamentarians against the Royalist army of King Charles I. For his pains he was captured and imprisoned first in Hasduck House in Nottingham until he was moved to Newark Castle. On his release he settled in Nottingham, married, and had four children. His descendant, Francis Wright, inherited property in Osmaston, Derbyshire, which established the Wrights as a Midlands family. Like the Fergusons much of their social advancement came

through marriage. They were connected to the Whitbread
brewing family, the Romneys, the Dacres, and the Dukes of
Buccleuch.

The Wrights were a prosperous family. Susie lived with her
two sisters and brother Bryan—later to become a butler—at
Bridgewater House, Grantham, Lincolnshire, where her
father was a well-to-do director of an engineering company.
She was an accomplished horsewoman, and it was among the
hunting set that Lieutenant Ferguson wooed and won eigh-
teen-year-old Susie.

While the couple seemed well matched, as both came from
solid, respectable backgrounds, their temperaments were
sharply contrasting. Lieutenant Ferguson was aloof, placid,
with a touch of arrogance. Susie was excitable, extroverted,
and vivacious. A contemporary, Jane Bradlaw, who was the
hairdresser to Princess Margaret and Princess Alexandra,
recalls: "Susie was always happy about everything. She was a
ball of fire, always laughing and joking. She would come
running in to the salon and chatter away nineteen to the
dozen. You couldn't get Susie to sit down for more than five
minutes."

This contrast has translated to the present Ferguson family, for while Sarah's elder sister, Jane, has inherited her
mother's sleek slim features, she has her father's stoicism.
Sarah, on the other hand, shares an uncanny resemblance to
her father but has her mother's exuberant character.

The Fergusons made a handsome couple as they stepped
out of St. Margaret's Church, Westminster, beneath a bridal
arch of Life Guards' ceremonial swords on a chilly January
afternoon in 1956. They spent their honeymoon skiing in
Kitzbühel, Austria, before settling down to married life in
white-painted Lowood House in Sunninghill, near Ascot in
Berkshire. They plunged into a life of cocktail parties, society balls, hunting, and polo, which soon formed the central
pillar of their social life. Ronald Ferguson, now a captain,
first started playing the game in 1954 when he was based
abroad with the Life Guards. One of the advantages about
army life was that this rich man's sport could be played

cheaply. There was something of a stir in Parliament when it was discovered that Major Ferguson was using the services of a certain Trooper Smith to help his Argentinian groom keep his stable of eight ponies at Windsor. Polo is an expensive sport, dominated by the Argentinians, where the serious enthusiast will get little change out of a £20,000 season. It combines that heady mixture of danger, camaraderie, and skill that men of action find so enthralling. For Ronald Ferguson the sport became an obsession, where much of the fascination lies in its sheer difficulty—"You've got to maneuver a horse galloping at twenty-eight miles per hour, and at the same time hit a very small bouncing ball through a goal with a long stick while your opponent is trying to hook your stick and ride you off. It's very dangerous, but the fact that it is so frightfully difficult is half the thrill."

Polo is almost as old as horsemanship itself, and legend has it that Hannibal and his officers played a ferocious version using the heads of defeated army chiefs. The English home for this essentially élitist sport was the Guards Polo Club set in the idyllic surroundings of Smith's Lawn in Windsor Great Park. The grounds, bounded by spreading oaks and sycamore and a colorful plantation of rhododendrons and azaleas, form a perfect setting. As a select group of lean, suntanned wives and girlfriends watch from the sidelines, the lazy drone of jets bound for nearby Heathrow Airport will occasionally drown out the sound of panting ponies, the shouts and grunts of vigorous competition, and the chink of ice in Pimms. Susie was almost the archetypal polo player's wife. Lively, whippy, and fit, she joined in the gossip and chatter as she watched her husband and other players, including Prince Philip and his polo mentor, Earl Mountbatten of Burma, in full-blooded action.

It was a carefree lifestyle with a shared love of horse riding and a growing circle of friends. A year after they had settled into the routine of life at Sunninghill their first child, Jane Louisa, was born on August 26, 1957. Just two years later their second child, Sarah Margaret, arrived, and her father noted with satisfaction that she had the same red down of hair as himself. She was born at 9:03 A.M. on the morning of Thursday, October 15, 1959, in the privately funded Welbeck Clinic in Marylebone, central London. Her Libran sunsign signified that she would be exciting, passionate, diplomatic, and appreciative of the arts.

Worldly cares rarely permeated the comfortable, leafy world where the two Ferguson girls grew up. Life was comfortable and conventional. While by no means rich, the Fergusons were certainly comfortably off with the means to employ a cook, gardener, stable boy, and a nanny to care for the children. The detached and spacious house was decorated with horsey prints and military memorabilia. "There were always fresh flowers in the rooms, and I vividly recall the sound of classical music," remembers one guest. The air of gentility was often interrupted by the yapping of Solly, the family's pet Pekinese. Sarah, bright, lively, and a bundle of trouble, soon squirmed her way into the affections of a string of nannies. Ritva Risu, who came to England from Finland when she was only twenty-two, has particularly fond and strong memories of the Ferguson girls. "My first impression of the children was that they were so well behaved. They never caused the slightest trouble. Sarah was always my favorite, she was just so good and gentle, even as a little girl. She was as quiet as a mouse, once her head hit the pillow she was out like a light." Ritva, who slept next door to her charges, called her "My Little Redhair" and recalls how even as a toddler she had a strong will. "Her parents could never make her say 'Thank you, God' after dinner, instead Sarah would only say 'Thank you, God, for my good strawberries' which were her favorite dessert."

The two sisters played well together, although squabbling as children do over their toys. A particular bedtime favorite was a rather careworn bunny called Mr. Rabbit. While Jane was two years her senior, it was Sarah who normally won in the tussle. "She had that strength of character about her," recalls Ritva. "She was much livelier than Jane."

Her mother rode every day so it was perfectly natural that the two girls should be introduced to the equestrian world almost as soon as they could walk. Sarah was gently led around the grassy paddock by her mother on a Shetland pony called Nigger before graduating to a larger pony called Peanuts. It is little wonder that one of the Duchess of York's first acts upon joining the royal family was to take on the patronage of the Blue Cross Animal Welfare Society, following both her own interests and reviving a family connection as one of her relatives had been an active vice-president during the 1950s.

A live-in nanny was an essential part of the Ferguson household as Susie and Ronald were often away on holiday, normally to America, France, or Austria. The girls received regular postcards from their parents, inscribed with the usual sentiments: "Having a smashing time, missing you all terribly."

In summer Smith's Lawn beckoned. It was here that Ronald Ferguson's friendship with the Duke of Edinburgh grew and he took over many time-consuming chores for his royal sporting partner. As a boisterous three-year-old, Sarah spent many a summer's afternoon playing around the pony lines, helping to tread in the divots on the field, posing for pictures for the family album.

The Queen, Princess Anne, and Prince Charles were a regular part of the polo scene and Prince Andrew, five months Sarah's junior, was an occasional playmate. At her tender age, though, boys as a breed were creatures to be treated with doubt and suspicion. No one, least of all Susie, thought anything of it, "They met on the polo ground—but doesn't everyone," was her now famous phrase. "Our families would meet and naturally the children would play, like any other children. They wouldn't really understand what royalty meant at their age. . . . They didn't see much of each other until they were older teenagers when they would meet at polo matches."

During Ascot week when the polo season is at its height, the Fergusons held open house at their Lowood home. While their parents were entertaining, Sarah and Jane spent time with their grandfather, Andrew Ferguson, at his farm at

Dummer or on the country estate of the Maharaja of Jaipur, a polo-playing friend. Prince Philip was a frequent guest at Lowood as were Robert and Philippa de Pass, now a lady-in-waiting to the Queen, and Henrietta and Thomas Dunne, now Lord Lieutenant of Herefordshire.

While Ronald Ferguson moves easily in Society circles, he is not especially enamored of cocktail parties and prefers to leave the dancing to others. He is a self-confessed fireside and carpet slippers man who enjoys nothing more than to put on his dressing gown and watch sports on television. "One has to go to a lot of these things, but I can't wait to get to my car and drive back home," he says. Prince Philip particularly enjoyed the easy informality of the Fergusons' polo parties, away from the stiffness of Court life. He enjoyed Susie's high spirits and she in turn was flattered by his attention. Susie used these social occasions to do a little matchmaking of her own. In view of what the future held in store it is ironic that it should have been her friends who often rang asking if she could fix up dates with the dashing polo players, especially the romantic Argentinians, who spent the summer in Britain. "I had a couple of very pleasant evenings with polo players Susie introduced me to," recalls one middle-aged party-goer, remembering those Swinging Sixties days with some nostalgia.

While summer was dominated by polo or holidays in the West Country, in winter the family went skiing, alternating between resorts in Austria and Switzerland. Sarah first put on skis when she was only four years old and showed her future character as she whizzed down the slopes. "She goes straight down—bang," says her father. "She always has done, not particularly elegantly, but dead straight." While Jane always looked poised in the saddle or on the slopes, she invariably managed to lag behind her little sister. "Sarah is a sporting girl, a tough girl," says her father proudly who gave her the nickname "G.B."—initials whose meaning he has steadfastly refused to reveal.

So it was that this young tomboy joined a select group of children at Mrs. Laytham's kindergarten in Englefield Green near her Ascot home. Her sister had just left the playgroup for the local Hurst Lodge school where Sarah would eventually join her. While Sarah was content to wear the white socks, gray skirt, and blue jersey of her first "Big School," she was happiest at weekends when she was on horseback. By the time she was ten her bedroom wall was covered in rosettes from gymkhanas and county shows. Her mother, who gave riding lessons to Sarah's school friends, has nothing but praise for her ability. "Sarah is one of the most natural riders you could ever hope to find. She has tremendous ability. When she was little I could put her on anything and say: 'Right, go and jump that' and she could. Sarah could make, or somehow will, the horse to do whatever she wanted. Sarah's just got that go." It came as no surprise that she represented her school at the All England Schools Championships at Hickstead—the mecca for showjumpers.

Just as his daughter found enjoyment outside the classroom, so Ronald Ferguson, now a major, saw his life changing directions. He was a middle-ranking army officer with little prospect of further promotion. Socially he was becoming drawn further into the world of the royal courtier. He and Susie were regular New Year guests as Sandringham and attended house parties at Windsor Castle. They even took part in an impromptu horse race with the Queen, Prince Philip, Princess Margaret, and several other members of the royal family during Ascot week. The choice between continuing his military life and switching careers was made for him when his father, Colonel Ferguson, died in 1966 leaving Dummer Down House and its eight hundred acres of mixed arable farmland to his only son. Inevitably Major Ferguson chose to leave the Life Guards, although not without considerable regrets, "I've had twenty years with the Household Cavalry and enjoyed every second of it." He delayed the decision for a further year before resigning his commission and moving into the charming, red brick Georgian home. Along with the move, the Ferguson links with the royal family became even closer. New neighbors included Prince Charles's skiing companions, Charlie and Patti Palmer-Tomkinson, the Queen's confidante, Elizabeth Wills, and one of the many girls tipped to be Prince Charles's bride during his bachelor days, Rosie Clifton. The Fergusons are respected locally. "They were always good employers, not at all snobby," says Doris Heather, whose husband worked for the family for over thirty years. The family links with the village were underpinned when Colonel Ferguson's widow remarried Air Marshall Sir Thomas Elmhirst and moved into The Cottage in the center of Dummer.

Upheaval at home also led to farewells at school for Sarah, who had just settled into Hurst Lodge. She was moved to Daneshill House as a weekly boarder. It is here where she made several lifelong friends, including Clare Wentworth-Stanley and Charlotte "Lulu" Blacker, perhaps the most outrageous of their present circle, although she insists, "I don't think Sarah needs any help from me to lead her astray!"

Sarah joined twelve other new pupils at the mixed preparatory boarding school which was presided over with maternal devotion by the founder, Miss June Vallance. Her philosophy on education is simple and has changed little in twenty years. She states, with conviction, "The aim is to make the best use of the talents the children have. I like to make sure that they have a relaxed and enjoyable childhood. Remember, adult life lasts a rather long time and can be very hard work." The daily routine was similar to many public schools. A wake-up call at seven in the morning, then breakfast of bacon, eggs, toast, and tea, and followed by assembly. Math, English, history, and geography were compulsory subjects and Sarah chose French as her language. Miss Vallance took more than a passing interest in the curly haired youngster who was called Fergie by one and all, and frequently visited the family home. "I remember calling one day to hear a 'thump, thump, thump' on the stairs," she recalls. "There were Sarah and Jane using an eiderdown for a toboggan and bouncing down the stairs. It was a murderous game that must have left the girls black and blue for days. But that was the kind of family they were, always good, clean fun, and full of life."

On one occasion the skylarking turned to tears when Sarah

(above left) Jane and Sarah (pictured right) with their doting Finnish nanny Ritva Risu who worked for the Fergusons. She called Sarah "My Little Redhair."

(above right) A delightful photograph of Sarah Ferguson taken shortly after her first birthday. She was born at the private Welbeck Clinic in London's Marylebone and spent her early years at the family home at Lowood, near Ascot.

(left) The marriage of Major Ronald Ferguson and Miss Susan Wright took place at St. Margaret's, Westminster in 1956. Major Ferguson's regiment, the Life Guards, formed a guard of honor as the happy couple left the church.

Sarah seated at her mother's dressing table.

The Ferguson family outside their home at Lowood.

Sarah, Jane, and her cousin (center) at Stonehenge.

Sarah and Jane were taught to ride by their mother almost as soon as they could walk. Sarah is fearless when she is in the saddle.

The girls take a break from playing "horsey" in a park near their parents' home. They used an old clothesline as makeshift reins.

(left) A chance photograph captures a childhood meeting between Sarah (far left) and Prince Andrew. While Sarah gives the Prince a winning smile, in the foreground Prince Edward and Lady Sarah Armstrong-Jones play on, watched by the Queen. Sarah's mother, Mrs. Susan Barrantes, recalls: "Our families would meet and naturally the children would play, like any other children."

The Ferguson family home, Dummer Down Farm, set in rolling Hampshire countryside. It was once used as a royal hunting lodge.

Sarah, aged sixteen, as chief bridesmaid at her sister's wedding to the Australian polo player, Mr. Alex Makim. After her wedding, Jane moved to live on her husband's remote family farm in northern New South Wales.

(left) A delightful study of Sarah taken while she and her friend, Charlotte McGowan, stayed with Hector and Susie Barrantes on their ranch in Argentina before embarking on a bus adventure around South and North America. Note the initials "G.B." on the chain around Sarah's neck. It is Major Ferguson's secret nickname for his effervescent daughter.

(below) A family gathering at Dummer, Christmas 1983.

Sarah cradles her half sister, Eliza, in her arms following her christening in 1986. "The Duchess will make a marvelous mother," says her stepmother, Susan Ferguson.

(left) Sarah deep in conversation with her former boyfriend Paddy McNally on board a luxury yacht in Cannes harbor during the Monaco Grand Prix. In the background is McNally's friend, Rupert Dean.

(below) The sitting room Sarah shared with her former flatmate, Carolyn Cotterell. Their flat in Lavender Gardens, Clapham, was a model of good taste thanks to Carolyn's passion for rummaging around antique shops for bargains. Invariably Sarah bought fresh flowers for their home—freesias, roses, and daffodils are her favorites.

Sealed with a kiss. Prince Andrew, who admitted he was "over the moon," pauses to kiss his royal fiancée as the happy couple pose for photographers in the gardens of Buckingham Palace on the day of their engagement, March 19, 1986. During their television interview the royal couple delighted everyone by their informal, lively relationship. "Sarah simply zings with life," noted the Press Association's Court correspondent Tom Corby afterward. "I can see why Prince Andrew fell in love with her."

fell out of the top bunk in her dormitory and badly cut herself. Miss Vallance rushed her to hospital in her car. She recalls, "Even though she bled all over the back seat of my car she never complained, moaned, or whined. Very courageous. She was certainly a character."

While she drove herself hard at tennis, netball, rounders, and swimming, it was horse riding where Sarah was her own severest critic. Her father recalls, "She used to take crashing falls, and she would sit on the ground beating it in frustration. That was because she knew perfectly well that it was her fault that she had fallen off, not the horse's."

The sisters' days at Daneshill came to an abrupt end when Miss Vallance's brother decided to sell the house and move to a new site at Dogmersfield in Hampshire. It was decided that Sarah and Jane would return to Hurst Lodge as weekly boarders, joining two hundred other pupils at the school whose motto is "Art for Art's Sake." When they arrived the most famous old girls were the actress Charlotte Cornwell and Emma Forbes, the daughter of film director Bryan Forbes. This cheerful, carefree school was run by the younger sister of the film actor Trevor Howard, who had met Major Ferguson when he was the military advisor for the film, *The Charge of the Light Brigade*, which starred the movie veteran. Indeed, the daughters of actors and artists proliferated at the school. One of Sarah's closest friends was Florence Belmondo, the daughter of French film star Jean-Paul Belmondo. She is now married to a Seattle property dealer but still plays hostess to the Duchess when she visits Paris or at her home on the island paradise of Antigua. For such an obviously outdoor girl, Sarah showed a surprising aptitude for art. Her art teacher Joe Smale recalls, "She had a great perception of detail. She was diligent and conscientious in her work."

As Sarah prepared to move up to her second year, her teenage world came tumbling round her ears when her mother told the girls that she and their father were parting after sixteen years of married life. The news came as a blow but not as a total surprise. Both girls were sensitive and perceptive and could see the growing distance between their parents. Susie spent more time at their town house in Chelsea while Ronald was increasingly immersed in his polo world. In 1972, about the time of the break up of their marriage, he became Prince Charles's polo manager—"I do it as an act of friendship," he insisted—and moved further into his own obsessive universe.

The rival for Susie Ferguson's affections came in the shambling, good-natured shape of Hector Barrantes, a brilliant Argentinian polo player who arrived in England in 1967 to star on the team sponsored by meat millionaire Lord Vestey. While this burly sportsman spoke little English, he was eloquent on the polo field, displaying a deftness of touch that belied his thickset physique. Naturally Hector Barrantes was known to the Fergusons, and they were as shocked as everyone else in the polo world to hear of his wife's tragic death in a car crash outside Buenos Aires. To compound the horrifying story, Louise Barrantes was eight months pregnant at the time. For Hector, who badly fractured his right leg in the incident, her death, after fourteen years of marriage, came as a devastating blow. As a way of trying to put the past behind him, he joined a party of polo friends on the island of Corfu at the end of the playing season. The Fergusons were among the friends who enjoyed barbecues on the beach, cruising in the Mediterranean, and lazing in the warm summer sunshine. Barrantes, charming, affable, *laissez-faire*, is a character in marked contrast to Major Ferguson's cool, matter-of-fact approach to life. The inevitable happened. Susie fell hopelessly and madly in love.

Although the divorce was reasonably civilized, Major Ferguson discovered that friendship can be skin deep: "A lot of people thought it was going to be messy, and those people who didn't want to be tainted with it buzzed off. These were people whom I thought were friends, but weren't." There is still a legacy of rancor even today. It is noticeable, for example, that when the Barrantes visit Smith's Lawn during Ascot week, Major Ferguson makes himself scarce. When he speaks of Señor Barrantes it is not with warmth. However, he insists: "Susan and I see each other every year when she comes to England to see her family. I assure you that our relationship from the time she moved away has been very civilized, and that goes for her new husband as well."

Financially the divorce was reasonably straightforward. Susie took a share of the family jewels and part of the proceeds from the sale of their house in Flood Street, Chelsea. The house had unhappy associations anyway. It had been damaged when the IRA left a bomb outside the front door. The device, planted at a time when the Price Sisters were languishing in Holloway Prison, was intended for the house opposite which was occupied by a prison warder. Jane and their housekeeper were in the house at the time but escaped safely though shocked.

Socially, however, the break was a mess. Barrantes was still a top polo player and Ferguson a senior figure in the game. Their paths would and do cross. Indeed just days after the marriage was dissolved, Hector Barrantes and Major Ferguson faced each other across the polo field. The match, between Stowell Park and Pimms, ended in an honorable draw.

Fortunately, Hector Barrantes was not only appreciated in Britain and was able to spend his time between Greenwich polo club in Connecticut and playing for printing magnate Peter Brant at the Palm Beach polo ground. While the Barrantes are a much traveled couple, dividing their time between Argentina, Florida, New York, and England, their first home together was in the Sussex village of Iping, near Cowdray Park polo ground. They married quietly and without fuss at Chichester Register Office in July 1975. Two polo friends, Juan MacDonough and Gonzales Pieres were witnesses to the union. There was one sadness. Even if they had wished, Susie was unable to have any more children following a miscarriage in the early 1960s, which led to further complications.

While both parents tried to shield Sarah and Jane from the emotional effects, they were deeply scarred. Jane now admits, "The break-up affected us both. We are still close to our mother though we never saw as much of her as we did of Dad following the divorce. When our mother attended Sarah's wedding it was the first time we had all been together for ten years." The emotional wounds can still be seen in Sarah's character. Friends point to her overenthusiastic desire to please, her craving for stable relationships, the underlying drumbeat of insecurity that is muffled by her relentless high spirits.

At the time Major Ferguson did his best to cope. He reacted with characteristic military aplomb and tried to pass off the episode without too much fuss. "I've never been an overindulgent father," he says. "I wouldn't attempt to compensate for the trauma of the break-up. I set out to be the reverse. I thought it would be a ghastly mistake to compensate financially or with things. I knew whatever I did I had to stand Sarah and Jane on their own two feet. I tried desperately hard not to spoil them, and I think I succeeded."

The crisis in their difficult teenage lives did bring the sisters closer together. Major Ferguson worked hard to fill the gap in their lives, organizing visits to friends, helping them to buy clothes, and spending time on horseback. But, as he says, "There is no substitute for a mother, at that age."

The girls each reacted differently, for while Jane became more quiet and reflective, Sarah was increasingly effervescent as though constant action and movement could resolve their unhappy reality. Looking back Major Ferguson feels that it was his eldest daughter who was affected most by the split, "Jane felt more insecure, but Sarah didn't openly react to her mother's departure, and I don't think it changed the way she was, although she was affected." He gallantly shrugs off the obvious difficulties. "There might have been the odd trying moment, but I hope the girls never realized how tough it was."

Certainly the problem was helped by the fact that the girls were weekly boarders at Hurst Lodge. Their headmistress Mrs. Celia Merrick recalls, "The separation had remarkably little effect on Sarah. This was really due to her parents. They made sure that they had the minimum effect on their daughters." Her mother's departure came at the time of natural teenage insecurity. Sarah was no different from any of the other girls in Peach dormitory. She fretted about her freckles, cursed her pale skin which burnt at the merest hint of sunshine, despaired of her bottom—"It's too big"—and bemoaned her failure to find a steady boyfriend. "I'm such an appalling mess," she would complain. A contemporary, Jilly Adams, recalls, "She was terribly insecure and desperately wanted to be liked. In fact everyone did like her, she was the nicest person that I met."

Yet Sarah is a long, long way from being a placid goody goody. She is still a pranks-and-practical-jokes person—of the sort that the royal family appreciate. At Hurst Lodge she was able to give full rein to her jolly, hockey sticks humor. Pillow fights in the dorm, apple-pie beds, and illicit midnight feasts, these were the usual limits of naughtiness. On one occasion Sarah and her friends smuggled frogspawn into the gym changing room and filled another pupil's blazer pocket with the gooey mess. Another time she was in the thick of a ferocious food fight, girls throwing squashy tomatoes at each other after they had raided the display for the Harvest Festival. "She was a doer rather than a spectator," says Fenella Heron, a contemporary and daughter of comedian Ted Rogers. "I remember that once she filled the sugar bowl with salt and fell about laughing at the faces the girls made when they tasted it."

Another classmate, Alexandra Grant Adamson, now a nurse, remembers, "We were all terribly bored in math one day. The window opened out onto a balcony and everyone threw pencils, paper, and rubbers out of the window. Then Fergie—I'm sure it was her—actually picked up a desk and threw that out as well." As with all schoolday stories, some of the incidents may suffer from excessive embroidery. However, the flavor of Sarah is there—high-spirited, extroverted, and slightly reckless, displaying many of the qualities we see today. At the same time she was kindhearted, caring, and considerate. "If anyone was taken ill, she would always be the first to visit," recalls one friend. "That's typically Sarah. Just very genuine." It was no surprise that, after being made captain of netball, she was voted joint head girl. Significantly, both pupils and teachers took part in the election, reflecting her true popularity. Mrs. Merrick, now retired, explained: "We had a great emphasis in the school on good manners. It really means caring and concern for other people. That is something which she had in full measure. Sarah was a thoroughly outgoing girl. Scholarly pursuits were not her favorite although she tolerated them cheerfully." When it was announced she was head girl, Sarah reacted with characteristic self-depreciation. "They have made you head girl because you are responsible," her father told her. "No, Daddy," she replied smartly. "That's not right. I was so uncontrollable they had to make me head girl so I would start behaving."

As head girl she used personality rather than position to get results. "Sarah inspired loyalty and girls would do things for her because of the respect they had for her," recalls a contemporary, Davida Smart, daughter of the circus impresario Billy Smart. She was particularly popular with the younger girls who turned to Sarah to help sort out their problems. "A sort of Agony Aunt I suppose," says one old girl.

A portent of things to come came when her friend Sarah Alexander left to go to Gordonstoun, the remote Scottish school where Prince Andrew was then cutting a swathe. Florence Belmondo who shared a room with Sarah, signed her farewell wishes in an exercise book: "Good luck with the boys!!!" As she wrote, Sarah was more specific: "Good Scottish (sic) luck!! Mind Prince Andrew, lots of love, Sarah Fergie (Ferguson) XXXX XXXX XXXX XXX."

Headmistress Celia Merrick remarks drolly, "I wonder if she would have attended to her history lessons better if she had realized that we were talking about the ancestors of her future family."

While boys featured in bedtime conversations—Fergie had a crush for a time on the actor Nicky Henson after she saw him in *The Taming of the Shrew* in the West End—they were only encountered at dances with local schools. As befitting these hothouse affairs, wallflowers were the most prolific plants, as the boys stayed in one group and the girls huddled in another.

If girls' boarding schools breed a certain hothouse insularity they do not, as a rule, act as fertile academic forcing fields. Hurst Lodge was no exception to this maxim and Sarah's academic results reflected this philosophy. As she says disparagingly, "Me. A-levels? Don't be silly." She did gain O-level passes in art, French, and biology with CSEs in geography and math. "Sarah did a lot better than me at school," says her father with a wry smile.

During her last term at the £4,000-a-year school, Sarah's thoughts were less on studying hard than on preparations for Jane's wedding to a lean, rangy Australian farmer, Alex Makim, who had stayed in a cottage in Dummer while he helped on the Ferguson farm. He had originally come over to visit his sister Sally and cousin Belinda Coy, who spent several summers working as grooms for Susie Ferguson. At that time Jane, slim and athletic, was half-heartedly undertaking a cookery course in London. But her heart lay in the country and with Alex. When he returned to Australia, Jane wrote to him regularly, pining for the rugged, cheerful farmer. While Major Ferguson advised caution, Jane was determined to see Alex again and insisted on flying out to visit him and his family on their ranch on the Queensland border. Young love knows no boundaries and she got her wish, excitedly announcing the fact in a Christmas telephone call to her father that she and Alex wanted to get married. Naturally Major Ferguson was concerned that at eighteen his eldest daughter was marrying too young, no doubt reflecting on his own early marriage. He pointed out, too, the difference between life on a remote Outback farmstation and the green and pleasant lands of Hampshire. Jane could not be swayed from her decision. Sadly, Major Ferguson's portentous warnings came to pass. In a very public and acrimonious breakup, the Makims parted after eleven years of marriage. The timing could hardly have been worse—Jane made her move to leave her remote Outback life at the height of the criticism surrounding her sister's decision to leave baby Princess Beatrice at home during her extended tour of Australia.

These traumas were, however, merely distant storm clouds. When the young couple married on a beautiful summer's day in July 1976, in a Dummer parish church. Her father organized a splendid marquee on the front lawn and 150 guests wished them well.

Sarah was delighted to be the chief bridesmaid to the sister she had always admired for her grace and poise. She wore a square-necked white and blue dress that gave her a distinctly naval appearance. It was a harbinger of things to come. . . .

3

A Bachelor Girl

Freedom—from the tyranny of the gray school uniform, from the regular diet of sloppy macaroni and cheese and multicolored Jell-O, and from studying for exams. The excitement of Jane's wedding over, Sarah started to plan her own life. She knew she wanted a good job, was ambitious to make it to the top but, like many school leavers, wasn't sure about how to do it. Sarah also had itchy feet, a yen to see something of the world outside the quadrangle of her Sunningdale school.

That particular prayer was soon answered. For much of that blazing hot summer of 1976 she had stayed with her mother at their cottage home in Midhurst, Sussex. When the polo season came to an end she flew to Buenos Aires with Susie and Hector and then drove the 300 miles south to their small ranch in Terenque Lauquens. This was the Barrantes winter base, where Hector expounded his polo philosophy to young horsemen who were happy to sit at the master's feet in return for work as hands on the homestead. Sarah loved the life, riding with her mother, helping with the farm work, and learning a smattering of Spanish on the way. Her six-month stay is still remembered affectionately by farm workers. "Everyone had a marvelous time when Sarah stayed with us," recalls Hector. "She has 'chispa'—she is quick and fun." While her mother can speak fluent Spanish—when she first arrived in Argentina Hector refused to translate conversations to speed the conversion—Sarah relied on smiles and sign language to converse with the locals. When Old Etonian Kim Smith-Bingham arrived at the ranch for a long autumn break before starting a job in the city, she enjoyed being able to speak to another English person. She had known Kim for several years through his sister, Laura, and they struck up a lively friendship. She found him "sweet" if a little immature, and he warmed to her high spirits and sense of humor.

While she was enjoying the South American sunshine, Sarah's father was sorting out his own life. For months he had put his own plans on the backburner as he had tried to guide and advise Jane during her intense romance with Alex Makim. Now that she was married he could devote more time to his own relationship with Susan Deptford. He had met this cheerful, chatty daughter of Norfolk farmer William Deptford at a cocktail party organized by Victor Law, a polo friend. As one friend recalls: "Ronald was feeling very sorry for himself after the divorce, and spent most of his time skulking in his tent down at Dummer. He didn't want to socialize and Victor spent much time persuading him to come up to London to meet new people."

Susan and Ronald's first introduction was only partially successful. She already had a boyfriend and turned down his dinner invitation. Having fallen at the first fence, Major Ferguson retired hurt to his Hampshire farm. It took Victor another six months to coax him out of his monklike existence to attend a dinner party at Susan's shared flat in Chelsea. That meeting too almost ended in failure. Major Ferguson, who loathes the taste of garlic, was greeted by the smell of that herb when he arrived at the door and very nearly turned on his heels and fled into the night. He need not have worried. By the end of the evening, Susan was captivated. "A very special person," she recalls. "The type of man who is interested in talking to girls and is interested in their lives rather than talking about themselves." The next morning Susan was intrigued and delighted when a bunch of red roses was delivered to her door. The card said simply: "Wow!" There was no name and after calling the florist she discovered the culprit. Susan rang Major Ferguson to thank him, only to find that he was rather reluctant to admit to being the author of this charming gesture.

The romance flourished after this somewhat shaky start, and Susan made her first visit to Dummer Down House to prepare for the Hampshire Hunt Ball. Jane was away in Kenya visiting her uncle, Bryan Wright, and Sarah was home from school, racing round the house helping "dads" to get ready and making sure her own outfit—she was allowed to wait at table—was neat and pressed. When Susan arrived there was none of that surly teenage hostility that can greet an interloper. Sarah was excited and delighted that her father was at last showing a little interest in the outside world. Over the next three years Susan and Sarah developed a close and warm bond, a sisterly rather than a mother-daughter relationship. "She was welcoming from the first," says Susan. "She was a well-adjusted young girl who tried to please everybody all the time." So when Susan and her father telephoned Sarah in Argentina in the middle of November and told her they had married she was delighted although not surprised. The ceremony took place at Chelsea Register Office with a blessing at St. Paul's, Knightsbridge, conducted by Major Ferguson's old friend Chad Varah, the founder of the Samaritans.

When Sarah arrived home at Dummer after Christmas filled with traveler's tales, she found a sympathetic audience in Susan. For Susan, who studied French at the Sorbonne, had led a lively jet set lifestyle during her bachelor days. She managed a chalet in Gstaad during the winter and the Sardinian villa owned by motoring millionaire Tim Rootes in the summer. Her only contact with royalty had been when she turned away a disheveled, unshaven traveler who appeared late one night at the gates of the villa while Princess Alexandra and her husband, Angus Ogilvy, were staying. The shifty "tramp" turned out to be the bohemian Prince William of Gloucester.

As Sarah showed a similar penchant for the slopes and the sunshine, Susan was the first to encourage her to spread her wings. And when Sarah went through the various crises and triumphs of her early adult years, Susan was always there on the other end of the telephone line providing consolation.

With the excitement of her South American visit behind her, Sarah realized that if she wanted to succeed in the commercial jungle she had to learn basic skills. She and her friend Charlotte Eden, the daughter of the former Conservative Member of Parliament Lord Eden of Winton, enrolled in the Queen's Secretarial College in Kensington. With two hundred other girls they became captives to the tyranny of typing, shorthand, bookkeeping, and cooking. Sarah and Charlotte were the first to rebel against the regime, their fine plans of success dashed on the rocks of practical achievement. Charlotte recalls those days with some amusement. "Fergie is very intelligent and like me was never cut out to be a secretary. We were at the college because we knew it was important to get some sort of training and we both managed to scrape through. I'm afraid we were both dunces at shorthand and typing. We sat at the back of the class and giggled, we couldn't help ourselves."

However, both girls realized that their parents would not pay for them forever and that they had to earn their way in the world. Certainly Sarah had no expectation of a large cash settlement. She received a "meager" allowance from her father and a small annual sum from a trust set up by her grandfather. The confidential assessment at the end of the nine-month course showed that she had managerial and entrepreneurial skills, but her technical ability was limited. Her report stated prophetically: "Bright bouncy redhead. She's a bit slapdash. But has initiative and personality which she will well use to her advantage when she gets older. Accepts responsibility happily." Technically both Sarah and Charlotte were failures, ending up joint bottom of the class.

Her exam results were shorthand ninety wpm, typing thirty-nine wpm, bookkeeping 87 percent.

As might be expected, this "bright bouncy redhead" was finding the enjoyment of the London social scene more alluring than the dubious pleasures advanced by Mr. Pitman. Life was fun. Swimming and tennis in the summer, skiing and supper parties in the winter. Weekends were spent with friends at Dummer or at the homes of their parents. After college they would congregate in a hamburger bar or café and go out to the cinema or spend the evening in a friend's flat. She lived with her cousins, raced around town in a blue VW Golf—a present from her father—and made a circle of girlfriends who have stayed constant to this day.

The personalities of Sarah's friends shed interesting light on her own character. Almost without exception they are women who are achievers. Invariably they went to schools which put an emphasis on manners rather than mathematics, *petit point* rather than physics. They dabbled in low paid, high prestige jobs like publishing, interior design, and public relations, or worked as chalet girls and high-class cooks. They have the dynamism and initiative to succeed without the necessity for academic qualifications. In some this frustrated ambition was realized in exotic travel, in others by starting their own businesses and using their social contacts to succeed. It is from this breed of well-bred, socially tough women, who have torn up the conventional social map and have undertaken a little exploration on their own, that Sarah Ferguson drew and continues to draw her closest friends and advisors. Sarah had kept in touch with several Hurst Lodge schoolfriends, especially Florence Belmondo who moved back to Paris to stay with her father. Her cousin James Boughey, the son of Susan Barrantes's elder sister Davina, was also in London as were Laura and Kim Smith-Bingham, who had now settled somewhat reluctantly into a City job.

Kim, the son of racehorse owner Charles Smith-Bingham, a contemporary of Major Ferguson's at Eton, saw Sarah regularly. They sent each other Valentines, he bought her red roses and chocolates, they quarreled and made up, they laughed at the musical *Barnum*, and enjoyed the wave of dance films like *Grease* and *Saturday Night Fever*. As a token of his affection he gave her a sterling silver owl as a mascot for her car. Certainly there was no question of marriage or settling down. It was an affair that blew hot and cold as Sarah jetted off to faraway climes. "If they had met later in life, it may well have worked," admits a close friend.

Her secretarial course over, Sarah and her father flew out to Australia to see Jane and Alex at their eight-thousand-acre ranch at North Star on the border of Queensland and New South Wales. The contrast between the Georgian elegance of Dummer Down House and the ramshackle remoteness of Wilga Warina—Jane's new home—came as quite a shock. Kangaroos bounded across the paddock, flocks of gray and pink parrots screeched overhead, and the front gate to the estate bore a sign in Spanish saying: "Shut the bloody gate." When it rained, which is rare in a land where daytime temperatures can hit 120°F, Jane put out all her dishes on the floor to catch the drips. However, Jane—now called the Duchess of North Star—was naturally delighted to play the hostess and demonstrate to her father that she was genuinely happy in her new life as a farmer's wife.

Sloane Square society it was not. They went pig hunting through the scrub, herded cattle, and Sarah drove the huge air-conditioned tractor round the dusty ranch. They did find time to attend several country hoe downs, drinking ice-cool lager and singing raucous folk songs. Major Ferguson even played a few chukkas of polo with his son-in-law at the newly formed North Star polo club. "She loved it here," recalls Jane. The only unnerving daily routine was the trip to the outdoor "dunny." Sarah was advised to check before she sat down and scream for Alex if anything moved. The warning was genuine. Snakes—Sarah's only phobia—are regular visitors. One evening Alex and Jane were quietly watching television when a tiger snake, one of the world's most poisonous reptiles, slithered from under the sofa. Alex quietly got up, loaded a rifle, and shot it. The holes are still visible in the living room walls.

Her month-long stay was over too quickly. Major Ferguson and Sarah departed from Sydney Airport and headed back to chilly London—and the cold realities of work.

Her very first job was as a temporary interviewer for Flatmates Unlimited, a flat-sharing agency in Earl's Court. "She was bubbly, helpful, good with people," recalls her first boss, Wendy Keith. The job lasted for nearly four months and during that time Major Ferguson used his own contacts to find her a more permanent position. An old friend from the horsey circuit, Neil Durden-Smith—the husband of television personality Judith Chalmers—had a vacancy for a secretary at his public relations company, Durden-Smith Communications, in Knightsbridge. She started her £4,000-a-year job working for Peter Cunard, a smart urbane executive who regularly organizes the Berkeley Square Balls. Peter, who has maintained his links with her, remembers Fergie with a mixture of affection and benign resignation. "She incurred my wrath by spending a great deal of time on the phone dealing with her social life, fixing up dinners, and nights out." But her energy, contacts, and application won his admiration. "She was totally reliable, thrived on responsibility, and was totally professional."

Sarah would arrive for work on her bicycle—regularly decrying the traffic as she bustled into the office, invariably late and wind blown. Neil Durden-Smith was impressed by her abilities. When she suggested her friend, Charlotte Eden, for a secretarial vacancy he accepted her recommendation and hired her. He recalls, "If I had a knotty problem or a difficult client I would always bring Sarah in. She had that priceless asset of being able to get on with all sorts of people."

As her bemused employers discovered, Sarah's social life was a hectic whirl. After work she downed a spritzer over the road at Mossop's Wine Bar and then went on to a private drinks or dinner party. Her bosses accepted her regular disappearing act each winter when she went skiing, invariably with Kim and his sister Laura, Shona McKinney, and Clara Johnston. The Swiss resort of Verbier—nicknamed Chelsea-on-Skis—was the usual haunt. During the season almost everyone they knew would pass through. At times the British registered Volvos and VW Golf GTIs outnumbered the local cars on the high street. Meeting places like La Luge, Le Phénix, and the imaginatively named Le Pub, often resembled a reunion of the King's Road society. Every ski company was represented and during the high season two hundred chalet girls were recruited.

For Sarah the attraction of Verbier intensified when Kim left his City job and started work for Ski Service, an American company run by Dale Anderson which sells designer ski wear. He rented a spartan one-bedroom apartment, and Sarah stayed with him when she flew over for holidays. They were a breathtaking pair to watch as they hurtled down the slopes. While Sarah is acknowledged as a brilliant skier, Kim was more than her equal. "Probably one of the best fifty skiers in Britain," say friends who may criticize his arrogance but have nothing but admiration for his skiing ability. Certainly he proved a hard taskmaster. As one friend recalls, "Kim would slide over a precipice and disappear into space, leaving Sarah at the top wailing that she couldn't do it. When he got down he would shout at her to get a move on or else she would miss lunch. So Fergie would dry her eyes and somehow ski down. Yet she is quite brilliant too. I've only ever seen her fall in very deep powder when she has hit a submerged tree or something." However, on Kim's meager wages of around £70 a week and Sarah's holiday cash, long visits had to be paid for by on-the-spot work. Sarah took jobs as a chalet maid or babysitter and helped Kim make extra commission by selling boots, gloves, and other ski wear. Each January they drove over to Klosters—the resort favored by Prince Charles—and stayed with Kim's friends, brewery director Peter Greenall and his wife Clare. It is an annual ritual Sarah has maintained.

During the Verbier season they were frequent guests at a chalet situated a short walk up the valley from their own cramped apartment. This was the eight-bedroom chalet locally known as "The Castle" and partly owned by Paddy McNally, a former rally driver and journalist on the magazine

Autosport. They knew him before his wife, Anne "Twist" Downing, died of cancer in 1980. The couple had separated before her tragic death, and he was left to look after his two young sons, Sean and Rollo.

During her late teenage years Sarah worked and played hard, enjoying life in the mountains. However, her plans to spend further time on the slopes after her twenty-first birthday were benignly interrupted by her father. At the party in October 1980 to celebrate her coming-of-age, he offered a different proposition—a ticket to see her mother in Argentina, and money to help finance a trip around South and North America. It was the modern-day equivalent of the Grand Tour. Sarah jumped at the chance and immediately asked her friend Charlotte Eden to join her for Christmas. She resigned from Durden-Smith Communications where she had worked for two-and-a-half years and flew out to her mother's *estancia*.

Her visit coincided with a major upheaval for the Barrantes. They had bought a one thousand-acre plot of land called El Pucara where the nearest town was a stomach-wrenching ride along twenty miles of dirt track, the proposed polo field was still half wood, half scrub, and the only means of communication was a crackling radio telephone. Sarah helped them move lock, stock, Labradors, and Basset hounds to the wooden "A" frame house deep in the Argentinian pampas. When Charlotte—Sarah calls her "Cha"—arrived for Christmas the girls decided to see Argentina from the peasant's perspective—traveling by bus. Christmas was made extra special by a phone call from a tired but ecstatic Susan Ferguson shortly after Boxing Day. She had just given birth to a daughter, Alice Victoria—her first child, Andrew, had been born three years earlier—and asked Sarah to be godmother. She was thrilled and promised to be back in April in time for baby Alice's christening.

With light hearts and heavy packs, the two girls set off on their great adventure. "I wouldn't do it today, it's far too dangerous," says Charlotte, who is now married to Mungo McGowan, Lord McGowan's youngest son. They traveled by

bus from Buenos Aires to Rio de Janeiro, sharing the ride
with peasants who clutched assorted chickens, rabbits, and
vegetables in roughly tied cardboard boxes. The roads were
bumpy, the buses barely roadworthy, and fellow passengers
often in need of a good bath. They passed the time by
watching the endless pampas roll by, reading a supply of
romantic novels, or writing long chatty letters home. "We
gibbered away at each other to while away the time but
strangely, we never got on each other's nerves," recalls Charlotte. They used a guide book to find the cheapest hotels and
failing that, slept on the bus. By the time they reached
Iguaçú Falls, on the border of Argentina, Paraguay, and
Brazil, they had run out of *cruzeiros*, the local currency, and
spent the night on the cold concrete floor of the bus station.
They used their knapsacks for pillows and slept fitfully as
street vendors selling corn on the cob peddled their wares
around them. Naturally the girls were awake most of the
night and by morning had worked out a plan to secure a free
breakfast. They casually sauntered into a nearby hotel which
offered its customers nibbly bits of cheese and crisps with its
drinks. After ordering two glasses of water, they demolished
the plates of cheese and hurriedly made for the next bus. They
borrowed money from friends in New Orleans ("The most
worrying time was walking round the back streets of New
Orleans. We definitely thought we would end up mugged,"
Charlotte recalls), before heading west to the ski slopes of
California.

They traveled by Greyhound bus to the ski resort of Squaw
Valley where they worked, illegally as they didn't have the
necessary visas, in a mountain cafeteria. As in Verbier, Sarah
did a little childminding and chalet cleaning. Then they were
struck by a minor disaster when Sarah badly damaged her
ankle in a fall. Fortunately, it was the end of the ski season,
and they had planned to visit Susie and Hector Barrantes at
the Palm Beach polo club. Sadly, Sarah was too ill to fly
home for Alice's christening.

When she did manage to hobble her way back to Hampshire, she needed to find herself a new job and a new flat. She

heard that bloodstock dealer Angus Gold had a spare room in his two-bedroom apartment on the Prince of Wales Drive that overlooks Battersea Park. For the next two years he was her landlord. "She always paid her rent on time and never left her stockings drying in the bathroom," he recalls.

Her second headache—finding another job—was solved in a traditional manner by answering an advertisement in *The Times* for an assistant in a Covent Garden art gallery. It was a short-term job lasting just six months but she forged a longstanding friendship with art dealer William Drummond. Mr. Drummond, who has been in the art business for thirty years, enjoys, as he puts it, "the diggery, diggery, delving" research side of the art world. He has a gentle, unassuming manner, but an unerring instinct for a good picture. His practiced eye spotted one painting which he bought from his brother for £150. He later discovered it was a Constable and promptly sold it to the Tate Gallery for £100,000. He treats selling pictures as a sort of dinner party, dovetailing acquisitions with the tastes of existing clients. It was a part at which Sarah proved to be a skillful matchmaker. "She was a super saleswoman with that knack of remembering clients and their tastes and spotting what might please them," says Mr. Drummond.

In 1982, when the lease ran out on Mr. Drummond's Covent Garden gallery, Sarah used the opportunity to head once more for the snow and Verbier. It was not the happiest reunion with Kim. When she arrived at his apartment she discovered another chalet girl, Sarah Worsley, had won his affections. At the time Sarah Worsley, a niece of the Duchess of Kent, worked as a chalet girl for Paddy McNally. Like Kim she was in Verbier for the season, and so it was inevitable that they were thrown together. Inevitably, with Fergie's frequent prolonged absences, her relationship with Kim came to an end, but Kim insists that the parting was amicable.

In his castle eyrie up the road, Paddy McNally noted the breakup and made a mental promise to see Sarah when he next flew over to London on business. He had always enjoyed her company, found her wit stimulating, and enjoyed her infectious high spirits. When they met in London, Sarah was captivated by this balding, bespectacled businessman who was old enough to be her father. For while Paddy was not one of life's natural pin-ups, he was a man capable of great charm, sagacity, and—a quality many women find irresistible—a roguish twinkle in his eyes. It was the start of a schizophrenic relationship, years filled with constant packing and unpacking of suitcases, racing to airports or hotels, anguished long-distance phone calls and tearful good-byes. While Sarah was based in London, he was flitting between Geneva, Verbier, and working hard on the Grand Prix circuit.

Sarah was now trying to make a success of her latest job for an independent video company called VIP. Her job was as a Ms. Fix-It, arranging shoots, dealing with clients, setting up timetables for productions. One job was a video film which extolled the virtues of the department store, Harrods. Film critic Sheridan Morley did the voice-over, but the film, like the video company, went into the can. "She loved the job," recalls a close friend. "Sarah was very disappointed when the firm went bust."

This hiccup meant that she could spend more time with "the Toad"—her affectionate nickname for Paddy. She enjoyed playing mother to his two boys, making them bangers and mash, and buying them silly joke-presents like itching powder and whoopee cushions. Sarah also played hostess to the now legendary dinner parties at the Castle. The guest list read like a who's who of newspaper gossip columns, and the talk itself was just as waspish as any column. A typical house party would include James Blandford, the heir to the Duke of Marlborough's fortune who has since been convicted of drug offenses; flamboyant businessman John Bentley (then dating Lulu Blacker); art dealer Nigel "The Rat" Pollitzer, who once managed the aristocratic rock group, the Business Connection; and Major David Waterhouse, an officer in the Household Cavalry and friend of the Princess of Wales. Other party-goers included Michael Pearson, the heir to Viscount Cowdray's publishing empire; Hugo Ferranti, a member of the electronics family; and property dealer Ben Holland-Martin, a close friend of Princess Margaret's son, Viscount Linley. In this atmosphere of often crude and cruel bonhomie, Paddy held court. While he entertained at one end of the thick pine table, Sarah played hostess at the other, using her conversational skills to further Paddy's career. At that time he was planning to break away from the Philip Morris sponsorship group, which arranged lucrative commercial deals for racing stars like Nikki Lauda and Alain Prost, and set up his own company to arrange prime positions for the placing of advertising billboards on Grand Prix circuits. He used his Grand Prix contacts and made a point of entertaining clients at the Castle. Here Sarah was invaluable, chatting away merrily to vital but often boring racing businessmen. As with Kim's ski job, Sarah demonstrated her chameleon character, immersing herself in the Grand Prix world even though she found the entire business deadly dull.

While some work was done, hedonism was the rule at Paddy's Castle. After a late breakfast of bacon and eggs, Sarah and her friend Lulu Blacker—who worked as a chalet girl—headed for the slopes. Paddy joined them for lunch, usually on the wooden balcony of the restaurant Ruinettes, before spending the afternoon on the slopes. Dinner was normally at the Castle, the favored drink vodka and bitter lemon, the food traditional English. Paddy regularly teased Sarah mercilessly, making fun of her frequent diets—one week the "no red wine diet," another the "potato free regime"—joking about her habit of eating from the fridge, and urging her to cut down on her smoking since at that time she was a twenty-Marlboro-a-day girl. However, Sarah was fully able to give as good as she got. Normally, the evening ended up in the expensive Farm Club discotheque where Paddy had his own table. If Paddy had been particularly outrageous, Sarah's usual retaliation was to spray him with champagne in the style of the Grand Prix winners. Guests still recall the evening she unceremoniously dumped a bucket of iced water over his head when he flirted with one especially pretty visitor.

It was an uneasy, uneven, and ultimately unhappy relationship, with more tears than laughter. Certainly marriage was discussed, seriously by Sarah but with considerably less commitment by Paddy. He cited the children, the age gap, and his burgeoning business which kept him constantly on the move. Left unsaid was the fact that while Sarah was obsessively loyal, Paddy had a roving eye. His Svengali influence was so strong that before she did anything she would always phone him for advice. "It was always Paddy says this, Paddy thinks that," recalls a girlfriend. "Quite frankly she was besotted with him and there was nothing one could say or do to make her see reason." There was little she would not do to please him. A jumper with a toad on the front was one of the first of many presents she showered on him. She arranged dinner parties, ran errands for him in London, often popping into the Marlboro offices to organize his business affairs—and always in the corner of her bedroom an overnight bag lay ready for the next reunion, whether in a London hotel or in a friend's mews house. "If I went to the moon, Fergie would follow me," Paddy boasted to friends.

The stormy, obsessive nature of her relationship with Paddy moved on to calmer waters when she found a new berth in London. In 1983 her landlord, Angus Gold, announced that he was getting married and that his flat was to be sold. Through mutual friends she heard that Carolyn Beckwith-Smith, cousin of the Princess of Wales's lady-in-waiting, Anne Beckwith-Smith, had a room for rent in her two bedroom, terraced home in Lavender Gardens, Clapham. Carolyn, blonde, demure, cautious, was a soft-spoken vegetarian who favored peace and order in her life. Sarah, emotional, headstrong, extroverted, lurching from drama to crisis, was a determined red-meat eater with a love of grilled steaks and shepherd's pie. Yet they forged a strong and lasting bond that helped Sarah through the next turbulent years. Carolyn, now married to baronet's son, Harry Cotterell, recalls: "In all the time I have known her there has never been a cross word between us. We always said what was on our minds. In the beginning it helped because we had different tastes in food and so there was never any danger of stealing each other's goodies from the fridge. I loved her feminine intuition. She would always know instinctively if I was feeling down and cheer me up."

Her move to Clapham—an area of London frequented by the young, upwardly mobile who cannot afford Chelsea or Fulham—neatly coincided with her latest and most fulfilling job. Paddy was the architect, arranging a meeting between Sarah and an old motor racing friend and former flatmate, Richard Burton. Burton, dapper and debonair, drove a Ferrari and lived in Geneva, with a flourishing fine art publishing business. He was looking for a London agent to oversee his British interests. Sarah nicely fitted the bill and was taken on, although at nothing remotely like the £25,000-a-year salary that has been mentioned. Her new position as commissioning editor and directrice as it boasted on her business card, perfectly suited her talents. It meshed her knowledge of art with her business acumen and ability to woo potential clients. Her new employer was an unlikely art publisher. Educated at the Prince of Wales's prep school, Cheam, and then at Wellington, he had raced Formula Three cars until a horrific accident at Reims in 1967 left him with 65 percent burns and a realization that there was more to life than fast cars. After moving into driver management he dabbled in property development, before seeing there was a market for high quality Swiss printing. The result was two Geneva-based companies, BCK Graphic Arts and Richard Burton's Skira, which he set up in 1980. Sarah herself rented a humble attic office next door to Sotheby's in the West End of London. All she had for company was a kettle, a vacuum cleaner, an answerphone, and a framed cartoon of her friends, the Prince and Princess of Wales. The sporadic nature of the work suited Sarah, giving her time to jet off to Verbier for skiing and to see Paddy. Burton was a tough taskmaster, demanding high standards. She did everything from being a liaison with authors and photographers to overseeing current publications and setting up new books.

Her proudest achievement was her significant role in the

production of a fine art textbook on the Impressionists called *The New Painting* written by the curator of European painting at San Francisco's Fine Arts Museum. Against considerable competition Sarah convinced the author, Charlie Muffet, that Burton was the publisher for him. The scholarly tome went on to sell 155,000 copies in Britain and America and generated nearly £6 million for the company. Her reward was the dubious honor of having her name spelled incorrectly in the credits.

As Burton's confidence in Sarah's abilities grew she was given assignments in New York and Washington and even visited Arizona to see various museum curators and galleries.

At Lavender Gardens life was rather more mundane. Early mornings were spent with Carolyn discussing the day ahead and listening to their favorite disc jockey, Graham Dene, on Capital Radio. Invariably Sarah's working hours were packed with meetings, lunch dates, and business appointments. While she occasionally cycled the three miles to work, she would normally drive in her sporty blue BMW that her father had purchased from Lord Elmhirst. Diets were the leitmotif of her life. The grapefruit diet, the protein diet, the low-carbohydrate diet . . . the list is endless. Ironically, when she was on the Cambridge diet she mixed the powdered mixture in a Balmoral mug brought back from a weekend stay on the Queen's Highland estate.

She was a member of the fashionable £400-a-year "Bodys" gym on the King's Road, where Olympic decathlon gold medalist Daley Thompson regularly worked out. In summer she played tennis with farmer's daughter Helen Hughes, then the manager of the upmarket gift shop, Halcyon Days. Sarah's evenings were not quite so frenetic, frequently spent curled up on the striped sofa reading the *Tatler*, or *Vogue*, or watching television. The long-running show "Top of the Pops" was a Thursday night feature and any film starring Paul Newman or Clint Eastwood—the rugged older man syndrome—were required viewing. Their elegantly furnished home, where the sitting room was dominated by a huge oil painting by Sir Ernest Waterlow, was invariably suffused with the delicate fragrance of freesias which Sarah bought from the corner florists. Indeed, such is her enjoyment of flowers that the Duchess is now patron of the National Association of Flower Arrangement Societies. One of the few regrets on her wedding day was that she couldn't smell the perfume of the thousands of roses which decorated Westminster Abbey.

While Sarah was at last finding a career that suited her character, Paddy was forging ahead with his own ambitious plans. He teamed up with Bernie Ecclestone, head of the racing controllers' Formula One Constructors Association and struck a deal whereby his newly formed company, All Sports Management, was responsible for the positioning of advertising billboards at Grand Prix races. This simple but effective idea has now made him a millionaire.

His relationship with Sarah contained more twists and turns than an Agatha Christie mystery. In the summer of 1985 Sarah informed him that the Princess of Wales had wangled an invitation for her to spend a week as a guest of the Queen at Windsor Castle during Ascot week. Paddy thought little of it, although he smiled at Sarah's excitement as she planned her wardrobe. He knew that Prince Andrew would be present and had shrugged off her chatter about her friendship with him, for at the Castle Sarah had never spoken of Andrew in particularly flattering terms. "Bumptious" and a "big head who thinks a lot of himself" was her rather damning verdict.

So Paddy was happy to drive Sarah the fifteen miles along the M4 from central London and into the private gravel precincts of Windsor Castle. He unloaded her suitcases, gave her a farewell kiss, and told her to have a good time. Little did he know that waiting in the wings was a fairytale Princess anxious to turn Sarah's Toad into a Prince. . . .

4

A Fairytale Romance

The Princess of Wales is an incorrigible matchmaker, who delights in waving her magic wand over friends and watching the resulting chemistry. It is part of her sweet and still rather girlish nature to take pleasure in the happiness of her friends and confidantes. Weddings are her special joy, when she takes a vicarious if naïve delight in the ideals of romance embodied in the ceremony. She has even broken with royal tradition to attend the weddings of those who have shown her loyalty but in terms of the Palace pecking order do not warrant her presence. Both her dresser, Fay Marshalsea, and a Palace clerk, Sarah Brennan, had their invitations to their weddings accepted by the future Queen.

Loyalty and trust, not position and protocol, these are the watchwords by which the Princess of Wales governs her actions. In Sarah Ferguson she discovered these qualities in full measure. Throughout her difficult and often lonely adult life, Diana has had no more stalwart friend and advisor than Sarah. Only her sister and neighbor, Jane Fellowes, together with former flatmates, Virginia Pitman, Annie Bolton—

until she emigrated to Australia—and Caroline Bartholomew—enjoyed a similar confidence.

Their friendship, which will become the most significant
alliance at Court in several centuries, began on the polo field.
The then Lady Diana Spencer was in the early days of her
romance with Prince Charles. She watched him unnoticed
when he played at Cowdray Park, near Susie Barrantes's
Sussex home, where Sarah was staying. The girls hit it off
immediately and when Diana was smuggled onto the royal
yacht *Britannia* during Cowes Week, the annual yachting
regatta set on the scudding gray waters of the Solent, Sarah
was one of the few friends privy to the secrets of the blossom-
ing romance. Naturally the two girls had been aware of each
other before they met properly during the summer of 1980.
For a start they were related by marriage. Diana's elder sister,
Lady Jane Fellowes, had married Robert Fellowes, the
Queen's deputy private secretary two years earlier. His
mother was the daughter of Sarah's great grandfather, Brig-
adier General Algernon Ferguson.

They had friends in common—mainly from Eton—and the
shared experience of a mother who left her husband during
their formative teenage years. While the Ferguson break-up
had been as civilized as such things can be, the Spencer
divorce had divided Norfolk society, ending in an unseemly
court case where Diana's grandmother, the Queen Mother's
lady-in-waiting, Lady Fermoy, had testified against allowing
her own daughter to have custody of her four children. It left
a legacy of bitterness emphasized by the cool and cautious
attitude of Mrs. Frances Shand Kydd toward her daughter
marrying into the royal family and once more taking a
leading role in society.

The girls were bound, too, by similar attitudes and shared
values. They had an irreverent streak that manifested itself in
the enjoyment of silly pranks of the apple-pie-bed variety.
Diana is still remembered by skiing friends for her innocent
practical jokes during a holiday in a French chalet as a
teenager. They have bright minds, sharp wits, and cutting
tongues when the mood takes them. Mutual friends sound a

constant refrain: "When you are with them you have to gear
up your conversation. They are very quick." While Sarah had
led the more exotic life, she is the conformist who loves
tradition, home, hearth, and family. It is Diana, the girl who
has spent her adult years cocooned in convention, who is the
erstwhile rebel. It is a trait noticed by a friend from her days
at her West Heath school. "Diana saw school as something to
be endured," she recalls. "In those days she was anti-estab-
lishment in a quiet, cheeky way."

During the early days of her romance with Prince Charles,
it was to Sarah she turned for help and advice. Sarah was
older, more experienced, and wiser in the ways of the world.
The telephone line between Diana's flat at Coleherne Court
and the offices of Durden-Smith, where Sarah worked, regularly buzzed with the latest gossip. "Sarah was very discreet," recalls her former employer, Peter Cunard. "We knew
she had royal connections but she certainly never broadcast
the fact."

It was discretion and loyalty that Diana needed after her
wedding at St. Paul's Cathedral in July 1981 at which Sarah
and her father were guests. When the royal couple returned to
Balmoral after their honeymoon on board the royal yacht
Britannia, Sarah was one of the weekend house guests waiting to greet them. Indeed, she became such a familiar figure
at Sandringham and Balmoral that royal staff never gave her
a second glance. "There goes Diana's friend," they would say
as she arrived for four-day visits, luggage piled high in the
back seat of her BMW car.

It was Sarah who was one of the first to know when Diana
became pregnant, and it was she who helped her through the
sickness and discomfort of those difficult months. Art dealer
William Drummond was then Sarah's boss and often had to
let her scoot off to Kensington Palace to help raise Diana's
flagging spirits. She was regularly called on at short notice to
accompany the Princess to the theater or the cinema. They
met for girls-only lunches on the fourth floor of the department store Harvey Nichols. In the summer they sat outside
on the brick terrace, sipping white wine, and eating smoked

salmon sandwiches while Diana's detective sat at a table
nearby. As often as her work would allow, Sarah saw Diana
each Thursday for lunch at Kensington Palace. Such was
Sarah's closeness to the Princess that she was the only outsider allowed to her twenty-first birthday lunch at Buckingham Palace. There was talk that Sarah was even to be
made the Princess of Wales's lady-in-waiting. The reason
advanced for not offering her this honorary position was
Sarah's age and inexperience. While this was certainly a
factor, the issue struck to the heart of their friendship. If she
had been made a lady-in-waiting it would have fundamentally
altered the closeness of their relationship to that of mistress-
servant, where one was always several steps behind the other.
While ladies-in-waiting are often drawn from the ranks of
friends, they are never Best Friends. Sarah was a Best Friend
who played a vital role in keeping Diana in touch with
ordinary life at a time when her new responsibilities and
position threatened to engulf and overwhelm her. One indication of how unsure she felt was demonstrated at Balmoral
where Diana preferred to slip into the servants' kitchen to eat
her light breakfast of coffee and croissant rather than face the
rest of the royal family in the dining room.

As in all strong friendships, the flow of advice and concern
was not one-sided. Long before Prince Andrew's green Jaguar was seen purring along Lavender Gardens, the Princess
of Wales's black Ford Escort XR3 was often parked outside
No. 40. She attended discreet cocktail parties held there in
her honor, and it was at one of these that she met Paddy
McNally. Diana knew the situation and proved a stalwart ally
during Sarah's frequent emotional traumas. When Sarah was
staying at Paddy's castle, Diana rang her, sometimes two and
three times a day. She had a code name, still used today,
although everyone in the chalet knew why Sarah was speaking in such hushed tones.

Diana, like Sarah's other close friends, had one wish for
the girl whose life seemed to be wallowing in a vale of tears.
She wanted her to be happy and realized that Sarah would
never find contentment, let alone marriage and the family she

craved, in the arms of "the Toad."

Ironically, Diana had tried her matchmaking skills before with her brother-in-law, Prince Andrew, and Carolyn Herbert, the attractive daughter of the Queen's racing manager, Earl Carnarvon. Carolyn, who was a regular visitor to Diana's apartment at Kensington Palace, saw Andrew on several occasions. However, the chemistry was lacking although they have remained friends. Diana and Andrew attended Carolyn's wedding, with Andrew making the headlines when he "goosed" his sister-in-law as they came out of the church.

Like Sarah, Prince Andrew has always had a special place in Diana's heart. They were friends and neighbors from childhood, and as they grew up there was a general expectation that Diana would be an eminently suitable bride for the Queen's second son. It was a thought lodged firmly in Diana's mind during her teenage years. At one New Year's Eve party at Sandringham, the Prince partnered Diana in a series of energetic Highland reels. On the stroke of midnight he wished her a happy New Year and kissed her under the mistletoe. It is no exaggeration to say that Diana had something of a teenage crush on Andrew and cherished fond dreams of marriage. They exchanged Valentines and Diana often mused with her schoolfriends on what the future might hold.

One girlfriend, now working in the film industry, regularly stayed with Diana during the school holidays at her mother's Scottish home and recalls, "Diana always spoke about Andrew, never Charles. She always talked about him in a nice, affectionate way. I remember her saying once: 'Wouldn't it be funny if I ended up marrying Prince Andrew.' It was a big thing with her. She would always giggle when she thought about the possibilities. She had a thing about Andrew in a way that she never had with other boys. In fact, she was usually embarrassed when we talked about boys. They were all a nuisance except Prince Andrew." These conversations were not just limited to schoolfriends. Rose Ellis, the cook at Althorp, Earl Spencer's country home, remembers vividly once teasing Diana because she didn't have a boyfriend. Diana replied, half in jest, half seriously, "I'm saving myself for Prince Andrew."

Since her marriage, Diana has enjoyed a robust brother-sister relationship with Prince Andrew. He has undoubted affection for her, regularly visiting Kensington Palace and staying for weekends at Highgrove. They both enjoy light-hearted conversational fencing and boisterous high spirits. There was an occasion at the royal family's Christmas party at Windsor where Diana and Andrew ganged up on Prince Charles. While Diana, wearing a pair of false plastic bosoms—a present from Andrew—over her evening dress, tickled Charles, Andrew tried unsuccessfully to debag his elder brother. This ribaldry was photographed by another member of the family, and the resulting picture is still treasured by the Princess.

Nevertheless, Diana sensed Andrew's underlying sadness and loneliness. He was a team player forced by birth and circumstance to lead a solitary life. "I have just lived a life quite happily on my own, and I make friends as and when they come along," he once said. The adjectives "lonely" and "reclusive" are frequently applied to the stark emptiness of his photographs.

For Andrew, at heart a home bird rather than the flighty playboy he has been portrayed, the path of love and life has been turbulent. His title has hindered rather than helped his quest for happiness. At school—like Charles he enjoyed the dubious spartan pleasures of Gordonstoun in the far north of Scotland—he played on his position. His reputation for arrogance and Teutonic aggressiveness followed him into Service life. "He played the great 'I am' all the time," complained more than one colleague during his training at Dartmouth Naval College in Devon. However, the orderly cozy hierarchy of the navy suited his temperament and he left favorable impressions on both ships, *HMS Invincible* and *HMS Brazen*, where he served as a helicopter pilot. On board he was known as "H," an abbreviation for His Royal Highness, sang the praises of Service steak and kidney pie and joined in the easy affability and insular "technospeak" of the

(above) Sarah Ferguson back where the royal romance began—at Royal Ascot. A year earlier, June 1985, Prince Andrew had teased Sarah, who was on a diet, by making her eat chocolate profiteroles.

(left) The Arms of Sarah Ferguson until her marriage. The thistles represent her Scottish ancestry, the bee is taken from an old Ferguson family crest.

The Duke and Duchess of York together with the Princess of Wales line up on the ski slopes for the now traditional photocall in the Swiss mountain resort of Klosters.

"My proudest moment," recalls Major Ferguson who watches with delight as the new royal bride, the Duchess of York, drops a deep curtsey to the Queen in the Sanctuary of Westminster Abbey.

The Duchess by the Duke. Understandably Sarah is Prince Andrew's favorite subject for the other passion in his life, photography. Even before their romance bloomed he once spent much of a weekend photographing Sarah at a house party in Scotland. He was captivated by her tumbling Titian tresses—although for this more formal portrait, taken at Windsor Castle, the Duchess wears her hair up.

The Queen and the Duchess regularly ride together after breakfast on the royal estates at Sandringham, Windsor, and Balmoral. Sarah has become such a favorite of the Queen that the Queen often refers to her as "my daughter."

The Duchess, the only royal lady ever to hold a private pilot's license, steps from a Bulldog stunt plane after completing her first loop-the-loop.

(left) The Princess of Wales and the Duchess of York are extremely close friends in spite of attempts to engineer fashion wars between them. Besides meeting to watch polo at Smith's Lawn, the royal friends go on holiday together, dine together, and even meet in the morning to go swimming in the Buckingham Palace pool.

(below) Prince Charles, who plays a defensive role on the polo field, receives a prize from the Duchess after a game in the rain at Smith's Lawn.

The Duchess presents a rock award to veteran pop superstar David Bowie. By all accounts, Sarah was rather bowled over by her meeting with one of her favorite singers. Her taste in music is middle-of-the-road rock. Elton John, Tina Turner, Phil Collins, and Chris de Burgh are the stalwarts of her record collection.

modern wardroom. The institutional life on board ship where the parameters of responsibility and enterprise are laid down and logged, found a convivial response in Andrew's personality. "You can ignore all that is going on in the rest of the world and get on with one's job," he once remarked. "When I'm at sea I feel about six inches taller." As for many fellow officers, the Prince found the Falklands campaign a turning point. He played an active role, his lumbering Sea King helicopter acting as a decoy for Exocet missiles aimed at his mother ship, *HMS Invincible*. The sinking of the supply ship, *Atlantic Conveyor*, and his part in the rescue of the survivors left an indelible and vivid memory of the horrors of war. It was the misery and chaos of the conflict, especially the dejection on the faces of the Argentinian prisoners of war, that inspired his love of photography. It was a passion that dominated his spare time. He even converted his Buckingham Palace bathroom into a dark room.

Andrew's love of photography has also provoked many so-called romances in his life. Helped by Californian photographic printer, Gene Nocon, the Prince was commissioned to do a book of photographs. He used several models and dancers, including Clare Park, Finola Hughes, and Katherine Rabett, as subjects. Inadvertently he was variously in love or in lust with all three. Such was Katie Rabett's discomfiture from the media that the Prince chivalrously compensated her by asking her to join him for dinner, which resulted in a short-term romance between them. Several weeks before that fateful Royal Ascot she played hostess at a weekend party at Windsor Castle attended by friends like travel writer John Rickatson Hatt and television personality David Frost.

Service and royal life conspired to ensure that unlike Prince Charles, Prince Andrew never had an overflowing list of potential companions. Like Sarah, Andrew remained loyal and friendly with his more serious relationships. Surprisingly for such a conventional young man he fell in love with girls out of his class, social circle, and country. One was the Canadian Sandi Jones, the other the American actress, Koo Stark. The quality he enjoyed about both women was that, because of their relative distance from the House of Windsor, they accepted him for himself rather than his position. Indeed, it was this lack of reverence that was one of the springs of his initial attraction toward Sarah. He met Sandi, the willowy blonde daughter of a Canadian colonel, during the Montreal Olympics in 1976 when they were both sixteen. When he spent two terms at Lakefield College in Ontario she visited him regularly and spent many happy weekends at the remote log cabin in northern Ontario. On one balmy summer's evening as they sat in the silence of the wilderness he asked her to marry him and run away together to Gretna Green (the Scottish border town that has made its name catering for young romantics who wish to wed). They both knew it was an impossible dream but it did not stop their teenage romance developing into a long-distance friendship. They corresponded regularly and when Sandi was in Britain she would see the Prince at Buckingham Palace. Similarly, when Prince Andrew made an official visit to California he made a point of visiting her at her home in Beverly Hills.

At home the Prince's naval commitments meant that he left the arrangements for his social life to trusted society hostesses like Ricci Lewis and Bridget Matthey. A frequent Friday night entertainment was a dinner party where the guests had separate courses at different houses before driving back to Buckingham Palace for pudding and coffee. Yet over the years he noticed that more and more friends dropped out as they married.

Besides his circle of aristocratic and former Gordonstoun friends, the Prince also mixed with theatrical, television, and photographic personalities. It was in this group that he met the actress Koo Stark, two years older than the Prince and infinitely more sophisticated. During the Falklands campaign they struck up a regular correspondence and afterwards they flew off to the Caribbean island of Mustique to stay at the cliff-top home of Princess Margaret. Their tropical idyll was rudely shattered by the arrival of several yachts loaded with the world's press. Was the royal hero about to marry an actress whose colorful career had led her into making several dubious films where elaborate costume was not required? It says much for the intensity of their relationship that Prince Andrew did not quietly drop his girlfriend after the first rush of lurid pictures and publicity appeared in the popular press. Indeed, she was invited to Balmoral and Sandringham where the Queen and Queen Mother were said to be impressed by her demure manner and vivacious sense of humor. The publicity was such that the Prince was obliged to wear various disguises in order to meet his lover. On one occasion he appeared at the home of Bea Nash, Koo's closest friend, dressed as a milkman. On another, as a traffic warden. There is little doubt that but for his position and her past they would have married. Prince Andrew helped Koo find her own mews house, near Kensington Palace, and for a time they secretly dreamed of setting up home together. But it was not to be. For once Prince Philip, who normally allows his children to lead their lives in their own way, felt it was necessary to ask Andrew to rein back on his headlong obsession with a woman who would never be acceptable in society.

For both lovers, this seering, searching experience left deep wounds. In Koo it was manifested by an unsuccessful marriage to Green Shield stamps heir Tim Jeffries and in visits to a Church of England vicar in Hampstead to have the spirit of Andrew exorcised from her soul. In Andrew it produced a wariness toward the media, a furtiveness in his relationships with other women, and an understandable reluctance to fall heavily and unconditionally in love again. The old adage, "once bitten, twice shy," was never more appropriate.

So during that fateful Ascot week in 1985 as Prince Andrew settled into his room in the George III wing of Windsor Castle he was less concerned about the guest list than his forthcoming visit to Canada. It was his first overseas tour since his infamous paintspraying episode in Los Angeles where he had covered several American photographers with emulsion paint when visiting a housing estate. In any case, the guests were familiar faces: the Stewart Wilsons, the Porchesters, the Husseys and, of course, Miss Sarah

Ferguson. She was there at Diana's behest but judging by the heavy-handed hints from his sister-in-law, Andrew rather got the impression that something was afoot. Throughout their lives their paths had crossed but always in different directions. At polo as children, at various country house parties as teenagers, at Balmoral and at Sandringham as young adults. They had first really "noticed" each other a couple of years before during a weekend party at Floors Castle, the enchanting Scottish home of the Duke and Duchess of Roxburghe. It was during his first flush of enthusiasm for photography, and he spent virtually the whole weekend taking pictures of Sarah. He was mesmerized by her hair, capturing her flowing auburn locks in dozens of images. She was, in the words of one close friend, "terribly flattered by all this attention but didn't really know what to do for the best." Paddy McNally and Koo Stark were still very much "items" and when friends pressed Sarah about Andrew's ardent if somewhat obtuse interest she was noncommittal and shrugged off their excited inquiries.

Perhaps she rather regretted being too familiar during a game of hide and seek in the rambling house. Prince Andrew had hidden under a table, and the blindfolded Sarah had crawled after him pinching his tweedy behind very hard. "Steady on!" yelled Andrew. "You aren't allowed to pinch the royal bottom."

Yet the boisterous element in their friendship was sparked off once again over lunch at Windsor Castle. He tried to feed her gooey chocolate profiteroles, she refused, playfully punching his shoulder and claiming yet another diet as an excuse. "There are always humble beginnings, it's got to start somewhere," admitted Andrew during their engagement interview. A week later he tried the same trick with a country and western singer during an indoor barbecue in Canada. This time it was strawberry shortcake. "He was just funning," said the starstruck young lady afterwards. "Just funning" characterized that wonderful week at Ascot.

When Sarah accompanied the Prince to the paddock to view the runners and riders, the headlines were predictable.

"Andrew's new filly," said one, and the signs of budding love clear to Fleet Street by the fact that two of Sarah's ginger hairs were on his morning coat. "No comment," said Sarah when tackled about a possible romance. "No chance" chorused the Fleet Street royalty watchers who argued that Sarah was not the same breed as Andrew's usual exotica.

They did notice that during his tour of the east coast of Canada the Prince was in unusually high spirits and was uncharacteristically affable toward the media. He even flirted with an attractive Canadian radio reporter during a private reception. While his good humor continued—he enjoyed his prize-giving role at Henley—Sarah was at a low point in her relationship with Paddy. They flew out to join Michael Pearson and friends at his whitewashed villa on the island of Ibiza. It was a summer ritual, spending several weeks lazing in the sun, swimming, and enjoying barbecues. Sarah joined in the fun, on one occasion cycling round the pool until, losing control, both she and her bike plunged into the water. The incident was photographed and subsequently appeared in the French magazine *Paris Match* when Sarah was engaged and trying to play down her links with the international jet set.

The thorny subject of marriage was for once avoided, although friends noticed that Sarah was less willing than usual to accept Paddy's caustic remarks. She gave him a frozen look and a flood of red hot language when he led the laughter after her bikini bottom slipped off during a high dive. There was no question of a break despite the fact that she and Prince Andrew were now rather more than simply good friends. The question was whether Andrew would realize that too. Sarah got her answer on Saturday, July 13 when he called to arrange to see her again—and the number 13 continued to hold a mystical significance throughout her romance.

Andrew took her to the ballet at Covent Garden, and they dined at Buckingham Palace. It was literally roses all the way as Andrew frequently sent bouquets of flowers to Sarah at her London address. As one of Sarah's closest friends said,

"Things got better and better between them as the weeks passed by. There was never any 'is it on or is it off?' It wasn't complicated because they got on so well together. That was the nice thing about it. A straightforward love story. . . . Of course, if Sarah hadn't been a friend of the Princess of Wales the situation would have been far more difficult in the early stages. She made it easier for Sarah to see him. You have to remember that in his position it is very difficult to meet women."

The conversations between Prince Andrew and the Princess of Wales during the annual family cruise around the Western Isles of Scotland on the royal yacht *Britannia* took on special significance that summer. Diana, arch, teasing, testing, happy to act as a go-between, probed Andrew to discover his true feelings for Sarah. It was an essentially conventional romance. Every Friday he would drive the 150 miles from his navy base at Portland to take her out for the evening. Sometimes they visited friends, or she would drive through the wrought iron gates of Buckingham Palace for supper. No dramas, no tears, no tortured confrontations. He had always liked her sense of humor. Now there was more. A lot more.

Paddy McNally was still a fixture and opinions differ as to when and how their relationship fell apart. One story has it that there was a tearful ultimatum over lunch at the fashionable Drones restaurant on Pont Street, London when she is supposed to have walked out after telling him that it was marriage now or else. Paddy emphatically denies that. Other friends say that when Paddy realized that Andrew was falling for Fergie he tried to woo her back. All are agreed that the last act in the saga was played out in the heat and fury of the Italian Grand Prix at Imola in October 1985.

The parting was adult and friendly. Paddy effectively threw in his hand. "Fergie darling, I love you but I don't want to marry you," he told her. He pointed to his age, his children, and his travel commitments. "What kind of life is that?" he argued. Sarah flew back to London to lick her wounds and think more deeply than ever before about her future.

Andrew for his part was playing a careful game. He arranged to have dinner with the television personality Selina Scott—she interviewed him later that year. She even replaced her tatty hall carpet in her Kensington flat in honor of her expected royal visitor. He visited the loud Xenon nightclub on Piccadilly with Princess Margaret's son Viscount Linley and his girlfriend Susannah Constantine. Sarah was not part of the group. Nor was she present when he went to see a radical fringe play at the Lyric Theatre in Hammersmith. The play's director Hugh Wooldridge, an old friend of the Prince, invited him and took along two theatrical assistants, Clare Fynn and Mandy Gough to make up a foursome. The photographer's flashes exploded and thus another romance was born. Ironically both girls worked a stone's throw from Sarah's West End office. Andrew also received a flying visit from his old flame, Sandi Jones. Always a royal watcher's nightmare, he was now playing a very canny game. Even in private conversations he would refer to Sarah as "Tracy"—a ploy which irritated the actress Tracy Ward, now the wife of "Bunter" Worcester, the Duke of Beaufort's son, the Marquis of Worcester, when she was quizzed by a reporter.

Sarah, too was more than equal to the subterfuge, although she was continually worried that the romance would make front page news. She and her flatmate Carolyn Beckwith-Smith had a well-rehearsed routing. Carolyn always traveled separately from her friend when she was expected at Buckingham Palace. Carolyn would check the roads surrounding the Palace to ensure there were no photographers lurking in the shadows. Then she would flash the all-clear to Sarah who would quickly sweep into the gravel forecourt.

While Andrew's desire for secrecy occasionally borders on the obsessive, it is a characteristic shared by other members of the family. It is one of Angus Ogilvy's proudest boasts that during his eight-year courtship of Princess Alexandra no outsider got wind of his royal romance. He still chuckles over the fact that on the day of their engagement announcement a book was published called *Princess Alexandra's Secret Lovers.* Mr. Ogilvy did not appear.

Secrecy was ensured by various weekend visits to the homes of Andrew's friends. The sprawling 130-room Floors Castle provided perfect cover for the young lovers. It was one of Andrew's favorite haunts. He had regularly used the romantic castle as a retreat during his relationship with Koo Stark.

Sarah herself found it hard to trust that her relationship with Andrew was going to work. Carolyn recalls, "Sarah knew intuitively that she and Andrew were right for each other and didn't want anything to spoil it. As a woman and as something of a romantic she realized this a lot sooner than Andrew. As a member of the royal family he is used to covering up his feelings. Perhaps that also means that it was more difficult to peel away the mask and find out what was really going on in his heart." Sarah's worries were perfectly justified. She had fallen in love before, only to have her hopes dashed. She was reluctant to be hurt again. This time, however, she had a staunch and loyal ally in the Princess of Wales who was working within the family to make sure that Sarah was accepted, and to make sure that Andrew realized she was acceptable.

Prince Andrew gave an indication of this family pressure when he was interviewed on television by Selina Scott. During an earlier radio conversation he had said that when true love came along it would strike like a "lightning bolt." When Selina referred to that bolt of lightning Andrew cryptically replied, "One member of my family, who shall remain nameless, suggested that perhaps it was time they saw me with charred ears, and I'm only sorry that this evening I didn't come with charred ears." It was the only clue he gave away during the publicity interviews for his book of photographs featuring the models and actresses who had been at one time or other billed as "the new girl" in Andrew's life.

Sarah must have enjoyed the private joke when Andrew was asked about the qualities he would want in a wife. "I honestly don't know what I'm looking for yet," he told Sue MacGregor on Radio Four's "Woman's Hour." "I've not had any chance to think about it."

Days later he and Sarah spent the afternoon with the Queen at Sandringham, joining Prince Philip for the first pheasant shoot of the season. That evening they drove to the 750-acre farm of Alasdair Hadden-Paton in Berkhamstead, Buckinghamshire. They spent the weekend together in his converted barn home, chatting and eating until late into the evening. The couple went for a walk around the farm, pausing to pass the time of day with estate workers. The game was very nearly up. A telephone call to a Sunday newspaper was made. They checked out the tip, established that Sarah and Andrew had been together but held back from running the story. The feeling was that Sarah was a cover for Andrew's real girlfriend. His false trail had worked remarkably well. It was not until a week later when it was confirmed that Sarah was indeed visiting Buckingham Palace that the *News of the World* decided to run the story.

When Sarah was approached, for the first and only time in her public career, she lost her composure. She denied all knowledge of Alasdair Hadden-Paton, of Prince Andrew, of the time of day. After a series of splutters and stutters she told the unwelcome caller: "I've got nothing at all to say to you. Sorry, I've got my boss on the other line, I must go." There was only one telephone in her office. Half-an-hour later she received another call from the same newspaper. This time she was all sweetness and light and prepared to chat about anything from the Princess of Wales's recent visit to Australia to the weather. The subject of Prince Andrew received a brisk "no comment" and the end of the conversation. In the intervening thirty minutes Sarah had spoken to her father, her flatmate, and her other confidantes warning them to say nothing and be on their guard. Battle was now joined. It says much for her own personality—and her father's experience of public relations—that at no time during the intense pressure leading up to the engagement did she lose her temper or her sense of humor. "I keep my head up unlike some people I could mention," she joked with photographers, making a sly reference to the former Lady Diana Spencer's habit of ducking before the waiting cameras. In some ways the attention was very flattering for her—"It was an immense shot of adrenalin," recalls one friend. "She is the kind of girl who thrives on pressure."

While her romance with Andrew was developing, Sarah was facing the biggest challenge of her publishing career to complete a book on the Palace of Westminster. Originally, Richard Burton had wanted her to organize a book on a royal palace, but she resisted any suggestion that she should use her friendship with the Princess of Wales to gain privileged access. Instead, she suggested a book on the Mother of Parliaments. She contacted an old friend from her days at Queen's Secretarial School, Anna Butcher, who worked for John Stradling Thomas in the House of Commons. Anna suggested Sir Robert (Robin) Cooke, an acknowledged expert on the Palace's history, as a possible author. Once again it was Sarah's charm and enthusiasm that convinced Sir Robin to undertake this daunting project. It was a commission that became a labor of love and demanded great courage. As he was researching the project, Sir Robin discovered he had motoneuron disease, the same crippling illness that eventually killed actor David Niven.

As Sir Robin battled on valiantly it meant that Sarah, besides dodging photographers, had to spend more time researching material for the book herself, tracking down photographs, illustrations, and source material. On one occasion she left her flat at dawn with an automatic camera to take photographs of part of the Palace to help Sir Robin as he wrote the text.

Her agitated state of mind was not made any calmer when very late one night she received a telephone call from Prince Andrew's former girlfriend, Koo Stark. Like Banquo's ghost, Koo had come to haunt her, to remind Sarah of her own affection for the Prince she had loved and lost. It was an unsettling experience, made all the more unnerving when Andrew admitted that he had received a number of calls from his former lover. On one occasion she had telephoned Buckingham Palace at least ten times in one day ostensibly for help in returning a mislaid passport. Prince Andrew, who is not the macho man he portrayed, sympathized with her plight and did everything he could to help her. "Like most men he will always come to the rescue of a damsel in distress," recalls a friend. However, these episodes and Koo's continued calls to the Palace—she used her code name of "Fiona Campbell"—did little to calm Sarah's habitual sense of insecurity. While an outsider may feel considerable sympathy for Koo Stark whose career and life was blighted because of her royal romance, this was of little comfort to Sarah. It is no coincidence that Miss Stark was one of the few former girlfriends omitted from the wedding guest list.

In those anxious December days she spent her life on tenterhooks continually worried that a word out of place, or action misunderstood could wreck her chance of happiness. Those weeks before Christmas also saw the final and irrevocable split with Paddy. She flew to Geneva and then drove to Verbier to collect the clothes and mementoes of a chapter in her life that was now closed.

Andrew too had come to a decision about his romance with Sarah. For the first time in a life spent in furtive liaisons he decided to drop the charade of secrecy and show off his girlfriend in public. They chose the Elton John concert at Wembley arena. The Princess of Wales went along to ensure that nothing went wrong. The threesome walked into the concert hall and took their seats. Andrew and Sarah made an elaborate show of kissing, cuddling, and holding hands, all the time waiting for the flash bulbs to go off. It was all in vain.

The next morning Andrew and Sarah eagerly opened their newspapers and discovered to their amusement that no one had taken any notice of their floor show. As Sarah's flatmate recalled, "She thought it was very funny. They did everything they could to be obvious except dance a jig on stage."

Oblivious to the mounting speculation surrounding his latest romance, Prince Andrew walked into the royal jewelers, Garrard, on Regent Street. He asked to see a few pieces of jewelry for a Christmas present. After a few minutes deliberation he chose a Russian wedding ring of three different golds—in upper-class circles the symbol of an unofficial engagement.

Sarah, too, had been busy and on Christmas Eve, as the rest of the royal family were making their way to Windsor Castle for the traditional celebrations, she called in at Buckingham Palace to deliver her presents. She was happier than she had ever been—everything was going smoothly, too smoothly. As she spent Christmas Day at Dummer Down House, Sarah took a long look down the road that lay ahead. As ever, her father's advice was shrewd and realistic, clearly signaling the possible pitfalls. The loss of privacy and independence caused the greatest soul searching. For a young woman used to catching planes like other people catch buses, the restrictions of royal life would be hard to bear. She had seen at first hand the daily frustrations suffered by Diana. Did she want this for herself? Was she paying too high a price for love?

The telephone call from Andrew was reassuring. He had had his leg pulled mercilessly by his royal relations—a sure sign that his romance was accepted. The Queen and Prince Philip needed little convincing about Sarah's suitability. They had seen her grow up, had known the Fergusons for three decades. As one member of the royal household put it, "Andrew couldn't believe his luck that he had chosen a girl whom the family liked as much as himself." With the Court on his side, there was no argument about Andrew's next move. When Sarah arrived at Sandringham for a four-day stay over the New Year, Prince Andrew first broached the possibility of marriage. Sarah was overwhelmed. While Andrew was anxious to get on with the whole business, Sarah was bewildered by the speed of events. For years she had considered herself the ugly duckling, the girl who was a loser in love, whose fragile happiness had always walked hand in hand with heartbreak. Now in the snowbound fields of Sandringham she was about to become a royal swan, to soar above those friends who, for years, had spoken of "poor old Fergie." She needed time to think, to consider. As one friend recalls, "While she was enormously happy, she was petrified about what she was letting herself in for." She asked Andrew to wait for just a little longer.

However, events had taken on a momentum of their own. The royal family were willing conspirators in bringing the young people together. The Queen invited Sarah to stay once again at Sandringham and the Princess of Wales asked her to join herself and Charles for a weekend at Highgrove. When Prince Andrew rejoined his ship, *HMS Brazen*, on January 19, 1986, before setting sail for Sweden, he took with him a very special photograph to adorn his cabin wall. It was a picture of Diana and Sarah sitting on a wooden bench in the Windsor Castle gardens he had taken during that momentous Ascot week.

Sarah's mind was taken off her own predicament by a joyous telephone call from her sister Jane. She had finally given birth to the baby girl she had always wanted. It had been an anxious wait for the Ferguson family, knowing that Jane had twice suffered the anguish of miscarriages well into pregnancy. Appropriately she named the baby Ayesha, meaning "gift of God," and asked Sarah to be her godmother. Just a few days later there were celebrations nearer home when Susan Ferguson's third child, Eliza, was christened in a private ceremony at St. Michael's Church, North Waltham in Hampshire. Prince Charles was a godparent, a sign of the growing family links. Diana once more played fairy godmother when Prince Andrew's ship, *HMS Brazen*, paid a courtesy call to the Port of London early in February. She helped calm Sarah's understandable nerves when the two girlfriends and Prince William made a ninety minute tour of the ship that had been Andrew's home for the last two years. "Keep smiling, for goodness sake's keep smiling," Diana told Sarah in a stage whisper as Sarah, wearing an outfit loaned by Diana, made her first public appearance with members of the royal family.

If the world didn't know before, they did now—this was the girl for Andrew. Even Sarah's mother, Susie Barrantes, tracked down to the polo field in Pal Beach, found it difficult to conceal her delight. "My daughter is very happy and having a lot of fun, the most fun she has ever had. She tells me everything, because we are very close indeed," she said.

The fun continued when Sarah joined Guy and Jane Roxburghe and Catherine Soames on a scheduled flight to Zurich to join the Prince and Princess of Wales on their annual skiing holiday in Klosters, Switzerland. There was near pandemonium among the assembled reporters and photographers when she arrived at the scheduled photocall wearing her distinctive Davy Crockett fur hat. Sarah was soon surrounded by breathless reporters, firing salvos of questions. She was friendly, in control, and giving nothing away. "Andrew is on exercise with the navy, protecting our shores I hope," she said before shrugging off the inevitable questions about the romance—"Boring, boring." In fact Andrew, on his last shore leave, had taken several friends for a night out ending up at Tramps discotheque, before setting sail on a NATO exercise—Operation Western Chance—in the South Western Approaches.

During her visit to Klosters, the Roxburghes had invited Sarah and Prince Andrew for a little peace and quiet at their Scottish home. It was an offer she was delighted to accept. The die was now cast. On Andrew's birthday—February 19—she dined with her boss Richard Burton while Andrew himself was rudely awakened by a fellow officer and ordered to make a practice flight over *HMS Brazen* in his Lynx helicopter nicknamed, for obvious reasons, the "Hussey." As he did so, signal flags were run up that read: "Happy Birthday HRH." This obvious sign of affection from the ship's company was a long way down the road from the days when he was the great "I am." Love truly had worked magic.

His ship docked in Sunderland for the weekend and Andrew, with only his bodyguard for company, sped off for his secret rendezvous with Sarah. She had laid her own plans with military precision. After having her hair done by her Scots-born hairdresser, Denise McAdam, at MichaelJohn, she dodged the waiting posse of photographers and caught a flight to Newcastle-upon-Tyne under the assumed name of Miss Anwell. Several Special Branch detectives were on hand to ensure she made a smooth getaway for her break by the banks of the River Tweed.

Floors Castle, the setting for the film *Greystoke*, is open to the public and much of its attraction lies in its sugar-coated Disneyworld appearance. After enjoying a boisterous snowball fight on the grounds and taking the Duke's Labrador dog for a walk, Prince Andrew got down to the serious business. The couple, as befitting a pair in a romantic Victorian melodrama, were assigned adjoining bedrooms complete with four-poster beds. As Andrew got down on both knees the absurd staginess of the scene did not escape Sarah. No doubt with a mock bow he posed the question that had been on his lips for weeks: "Darling, will you marry me?" She accepted with alacrity, laughing, "If you wake up tomorrow morning, you can tell me it's all a huge joke." He was deadly serious and to prove it broke his teetotaler rule to toast their happiness with a bottle of vintage champagne.

Now the planning had to begin amidst total secrecy. Andrew had already mapped out his ideas for the ring. It had to be a ruby to complement the cascading tresses that had captivated him for years. As for the dress, well, Sarah already had a few ideas in mind. She had previously admired the Duchess of Roxburghe's wedding gown, designed by Bill Pashley and on show in the Castle's public rooms. During the next tension-filled weeks she was thankful for her old school ties. Her flatmate, Carolyn Beckwith-Smith had chosen a dressmaker, Polish-born Lindka Cierach, for her own wedding gown. Lindka, who trained with Valentino and Yuki, had made dresses for the Duchess of Westminster and the ex-Queen of Greece, and gorgeous wedding gowns for Lady Rose Cecil and Pandora Stevens, the daughter of the one-time newspaper executive turned Rector of the Royal College of Art, Jocelyn Stevens. Her attention to detail—the fine beading, the shape of the silhouette, and the finish—were features which immediately impressed Sarah when they met at her studio. Her background—she had worked as a secretary for *Vogue*, traveled extensively in Kenya and, as an added eccentricity, wore a jumpsuit once used by a body-

guard to the Sultan of Oman—struck a chord with Sarah.
She was instantly marked down as one of her Real Women.

Sarah had an initial meeting with Lindka and, advised by
Diana, passed on to her a series of tips to ensure total
security for the making of the dress of the year. These
included extra locks, blinds on the workshop windows to
stop snoopers, and all material to be saved rather than
thrown into the dustbins in the backyard. Sarah also had to
start thinking more seriously about her whole wardrobe. The
friendly but featureless layered, Laura Ashley look of cardi-
gans and long skirts was not appropriate for her new position. Nor could she endlessly borrow from the Princess of
Wales. Here again her friends proved invaluable. As she
prepared for her own wedding, Carolyn had been assisting
her friend, Edina Ronay, the dress designer daughter of the
food guide gourmet, Egon Ronay. She was dragooned in to
help and advise.

Sarah's friend Lulu Blacker also pitched in. She lived in
Battersea with Susannah Constantine, Viscount Linley's
girlfriend. Susannah worked for the fashion house Ague-
cheek, which handled an up-and-coming designer, Alistair
Blair, whose neat tailored look appealed to both Andrew and
Sarah.

If Sarah had ever needed her friends it was now as her West
End office came under siege. One evening she walked out to
be confronted by a battery of television cameras and flash-
bulbs. Her former boss, William Drummond, happened to
be walking by when he spotted the commotion. He saw Sarah
sinking in the sea of faces, put his arm around her, and
dragged her into Sotheby's next door. They neatly evaded
their pursuers, and the next morning William was rewarded
with a telephone call from Sarah asking him if he had seen
himself on television.

Andrew took a starring role in another television spectacular when his shipmates said a theatrical farewell as he left
HMS Brazen. As he formally said goodbye to the officers of
the flight deck the door of the hangar lifted, and a chorus
line of sailors in humorous flying hats launched into their

own rendition of the tune "I'm the King of the Jungle" from the Disney film "The Jungle Book." One verse went: "I'm the Prince of the Hussey, an airborne VIP—I'm over the top, I've had to stop, and that's what's bothering me." The night before, as duty officer, he had conducted a poker-faced inspection of a dozen marines dressed variously in garter belts, baby doll nighties, and suspender belts and stockings.

Deciding upon the engagement ring took precedence over a number of official royal duties awaiting him. With true military precision he had a number of sketches illustrating his own ideas, and with help from what he termed "engineers" at the Crown jewelers, Garrard, the ring was made in just under a week. The fine oval Burma ruby with ten drop diamonds set in a cluster and mounted in eighteen carat white and yellow gold was left in a vault at Garrard for safekeeping.

As the couple waited for the Queen and Prince Philip to return from a three-week trip to Nepal and Australia, Sarah remained in close touch with her father, her stepmother, and the Princess of Wales. She even took sanctuary for the night at Kensington Palace from the waiting groups of reporters and photographers who dogged her every move. Her father was scheduled to travel to Australia to see Jane and his latest grandchild. As a precaution he had given a series of interviews with newspaper and radio stations on the strict understanding that they would not be released until an official announcement was made. He gave similar instructions to Sarah's old schools. They didn't have long to wait. On Saturday, March 15, Sarah neatly evaded the media corps waiting outside Dummer Down House and drove to meet the Queen at Windsor Castle.

This was where it had all begun just eight short months ago. Then Paddy McNally had driven her through the gates, but now Sarah drove herself in her father's red BMW using the private roads in Windsor Park. Over lunch the Queen was delighted to give her formal assent to the union. All that remained was for Andrew to speak to Major Ferguson and ask for his daughter's hand in marriage. "That was fairly nerve-racking, knowing Major Ronald from a very long time ago," admitted Andrew. Then, as Budget Day fell on a Tuesday, it was agreed with Downing Street to postpone the announcement of the engagement until the Wednesday.

Sarah arrived for work as usual on Monday morning although this time with a police escort. "I'm not saying anything, but it is a lovely day," she smiled. She met her father at Claridge's for lunch before going on to a fashion show at the Ritz—where Alistair Blair's autumn and winter fashions were on display. Susannah Constantine made the formal introductions, and Sarah explained that she wanted a suit for a rather special day. Secrecy and urgency were essential. Blair, who studied under Dior in Paris, was a relative unknown who was flattered to be asked. His team of dressmakers worked through the night to finish the distinctive blue wool crêpe suit with a pleated skirt, wide leather belt, and beaten silver buttons.

The couple had agreed that for the sake of security Sarah should now move into Buckingham Palace. It was something of a relief after months of interminable inquiries from the media who called her Clapham house at all hours of the day and night. Susan Ferguson—introduced by Sarah as "my wicked stepmother"—helped her pack. As she loaded her blue BMW for the drive to Buckingham Palace, she embarked on a journey into a new life.

The biggest day in Sarah Ferguson's life—March 19, 1986—did not dawn brightly. She awoke with a crashing headache and could only manage to nibble two sausages and sip a cup of coffee while her stylist, Denise McAdam, did her hair. The waiting, the worry, and the secrecy were all over as the Royal engagement was officially announced.

She and Andrew were in boisterous high spirits as the four accredited Court correspondents were ushered in to his study. Straight-faced he told them, "I'm glad you are all here. I asked Shea (the then Press Secretary to the Queen) to get all you Court correspondents together. I wanted to tell you it's all off. It's just a hoax." A touch heavy-handed, but the remark set the tone for the interviews to come. Businesslike, confident, and informal—a couple happy and relaxed in each other's company. Sarah, compared unfairly to the Princess of Wales and her engagement day interview, was controlled and in command, referring to Andrew only when she thought she might overstep that invisible line of royal propriety and reveal too many secrets about their romance. She liked his "wit and charm" but did not think she was that famous streak of lightning Andrew had alluded to in an earlier interview. "We're good friends—a good team. Quite happy—very happy." The characteristic clipped speech would have not sounded out of place in a wardroom briefing. Several times Sarah emphasized that "we" aspect of the relationship. The great "I am" was no longer. Marriage was emphatically a team sport, and Sarah showed that she was to be an equal player. The couple were determined to carry on with their respective careers, and they looked forward to briskly getting the business of the wedding out of the way as soon as possible so that they could settle down to a life together.

The Press Association's Court Correspondent Tom Corby was impressed. "She zings," he said. "She absolutely sparkles; I can see why Andrew fell in love with her. They were a double act, two royal jokers in the royal pack. . . . There was an air of restrained knockabout during the entire interview." As they posed for photographers on the lawns of Buckingham Palace, "Could you give Sarah a peck on the cheek?" asked one cameraman. "Certainly not," replied Andrew. "Oh, why not?" said Sarah, and then did it again for luck.

As Dummer church bells pealed in celebration, Sarah's stepmother watched the news bulletins and clasped her hands with delight at her performance. Before he boarded his flight to Australia, Major Ferguson described himself as feeling "reasonably emotional" and praised his daughter's cool calm during the months of mounting media pressure. "She is a very sweet girl, a very kind girl with a great deal of commonsense. She attempts to enjoy life to the full," he said. "We all know he's a professional helicopter pilot, and I admire anybody who is professional at their job."

While he set off to see his daughter Jane, and Andrew and Sarah enjoyed their first lunch together as an engaged couple, a nondescript van backed outside 40 Lavender Gardens, and several overalled men stepped out. They were on official business and a rather startled Carolyn Beckwith-Smith let them into her house. For the next couple of hours these courteous but brisk officials—from M15, the Special Branch, no one to this day knows—went through the house from top to bottom. Anything remotely connected with Sarah was packed away and loaded onto the van. The odd skirt, the silly Balmoral mug she had left behind, her duvet, anything and everything. Carolyn was allowed to keep one photograph in her album which showed herself sitting with Prince Andrew. Any photographs of Sarah were politely but firmly removed.

This was the Establishment in action. Sarah Margaret Ferguson was no more. She had stepped over to the other side. The wrought iron gates of Buckingham Palace were now shut behind her. They were her protection and her prison. From now on there was no turning back.

5

A Family Affair

It was a family affair. A celebration of tradition and continuity, an enchanting tableau watched on television by millions around the world. The marriage of Sarah Margaret Ferguson to His Royal Highness Prince Andrew Albert Christian Edward at Westminster Abbey on July 23, 1986, certainly lived up to expectations.

It was a moving spectacle made intimate by the human dimension, the personal touches resonating with the pomp and pageantry—the expression of happiness on Sarah's face as she curtsied to the Queen; her stagey wink to her stalwart friend Carolyn Cotterell as she and Andrew walked down the aisle; the Princess of Wales's tension as she willed Prince William to behave during the service; the Queen's protective hand on her grandson's shoulder as William chased the royal honeymooners as their carriage rattled away from Buckingham Palace. The scenes played out of the cameras' range and earshot merely added to the richness of the day, like Major Ferguson's rapture when he first glimpsed his "smelly little daughter" in her exquisite wedding dress at Clarence

House, and her own nervous joviality when she spoke to
Andrew in the Abbey: "I've forgotten to pack my tooth-
brush," she told him.

Guests spoke of the informality, the friendliness and
praised Sarah, the principal architect of the occasion, for her
creative attention to detail.

She could but have dreamed of the finished scene when she
and her dressmaker, Lindka Cierach, sat down with a sketch
pad in her light and airy Fulham drawing room. From the
start Sarah was clear about the tone and style of her big day.
It was going to be *her* wedding, a traditional union of two
essentially military families, not some blandly formal affair
engineered by a royal committee. Lindka's inspired artistry
brilliantly reflected those ideals in her wedding dress. The
intricate beadwork on the ivory duchess satin dress was based
on Sarah's coat of arms—a honey bee on a thistle tied with a
ribbon and incorporating the "S" for Sarah. This theme was
interwoven with anchors, waves, and hearts on the 17½-foot
train—an idea that came to Lindka in a dream one night.
Sarah suggested incorporating helicopters and teddy bears
but this notion was grounded. Instead the design was sur-
mounted with an heraldic "A" and "S." Naturally, Sarah's
trademark—the bow—was central to the theme. On the back
of the dress was a fan-shaped bow and there were further
bows at the shoulders. Like the preparations for the wedding
day itself, the dress evolved over a number of weeks. Endless
fittings, adjustments, and decisions—"I've got used to standing for hours with pins all over the place," she joked just
before the wedding.

For Sarah those first few weeks following the engagement
went by in a blur of decision-making. Life had a curious
dream-like quality, vivid and exciting but with occasional
hints of nightmare. She had long observed the Princess of
Wales and Prince Andrew performing their royal duties
rather like a spectator idly watching a fairground roller-
coaster and smiling at the screams of the passengers. Now
she found herself strapped in on a ride without end. It was a
very different sensation indeed.

In the months before the wedding she took over the suite of rooms on the second floor of Buckingham Palace once occupied by Lady Diana Spencer. At first she was so excited by the change in her lifestyle that she insisted on taking her early visitors on mini-explorations of her new home. The endless red carpeted corridors, the mute displays of Meissen china and Fabergé eggs, the pleasant courtesies of the staff— she was now heir to this heritage. No longer did she cook a couple of rashers of bacon under a reluctant Tricity grill in Clapham. Now she chose from a printed menu book each week. She was surrounded by staff and Prince Andrew asked his valet, Michael Perry, to help her settle into her suite. The Queen's chief maid Caroline Terry, a Liverpool girl who had been with Her Majesty for four years, was offered and accepted the position as Sarah's dresser.

Sarah insisted on keeping her life as normal as possible, spending the first week of her engagement visiting friends and relations—including the Princess of Wales and her grandmothers to show off her ring. The day after the engagement she returned to work bravely telling reporters: "I'm not going to change, why should I?"

However, her fine resolve evaporated in the glare of publicity. Slowly the shades of the Palace walls closed around her. Perhaps the first glimmer of apprehension of the growing shadows of royal life came during her meeting with Assistant Commissioner John Cracknell, Scotland Yard's head of the Royalty Protection Squad. It was nothing too alarming, a few sensible safety rules, an introduction to her own bodyguards, and a general explanation of the "envelope theory" of close protection, where one highly trained officer takes charge of the royal personage. This contrasts with the Americans who swamp VIPs with Secret Service agents, a practice scorned by Scotland Yard. Sarah knew roughly what to expect. She realized, too, that she would have to undertake an advanced driving course on the police skid pan at Hendon in north London. Bodyguards never drive their royal charges, allowing them to act quickly in case of an attack or other emergency. This chilling reality where she had become a possible target for an anonymous terrorist or an unknown madman didn't bear too much thinking about. However, Sarah knew now that an invisible veil separated her from her father, her family, and her friends.

Characteristically, she behaved sensibly and practically in the face of insurmountable argument. Her cozy fourth floor West End office was the first victim. Within twenty-four hours she was working from a study overlooking the Mall at Buckingham Palace. Her distinctive blue BMW car was the second casualty. The royal family have a generous leasing arrangement with several British motor manufacturers. It allows Scotland Yard technicians to install essential sophisticated radio equipment and also shows the royal family driving the flag. Sarah opted for a sporty Jaguar XJS so the swap wasn't too hard to bear!

Rather more difficult to accept were some of the letters sent to the Palace following the engagement. While the overwhelming majority were delighted with Andrew's choice, there was a minority, uncomfortably large, who felt Sarah's previous lovers made her unfit to be a royal bride. Many of the letters were anonymous, most were sifted out by the Palace clerks. Some did land on her desk and they hurt. These were not the professional newspaper bitches but ordinary royalists with an old-fashioned but unfair opinion of the acceptable background for a future Princess. One rule for a man, another for a woman. "You can't win," argued her father. "If she hadn't had any boyfriends people would say: 'What does Andrew see in her?' "

It was merely a foretaste of the onslaught to come. Just two weeks after the engagement, the fashion critics began to hurl their coiled barbs. American fashion writers were first into the assault. One bitched: "Forget the diamond tiara, this woman needs an iron." Sarah was called variously "frumpy" and "dowdy" and her hair, the crowning glory that Andrew so admired, was slated as "common and ordinary." The criticism of her figure and her dress sense was a constant albeit expected refrain until the wedding. "Here comes the bride, forty-two inches wide" was typical of the headlines.

Sarah, a woman who genuinely wants to be liked, was wounded and tearful, seeking comfort from Prince Andrew and her father, who led the counterattack. "The public knows Sarah is an ordinary person and is trying her best to be natural and herself," he said. "People probably don't like reading the unkind headlines and are saying: 'What the hell with it, leave her alone.' "

Prince Andrew was positive in his support and advised her not to read the attacks and to choose fashions that pleased her, not fashion editors. Together they went through her wardrobe, throwing out many clothes, saving others to give to Sarah's sister, Jane. "For the first few weeks I rather ran her wardrobe," recalls Andrew. Fashion had never been Sarah's strong suit. She admits, "Clothes are not a priority for me. It is a bit of a grind. I am not a great clothes horse but it is a job and it has got to be done."

Her friends also rallied round. Lucy Dickens, the fashion and beauty editor of *Brides* magazine, offered to help her, picking out potential designers and pointing out possible pitfalls. Edina Ronay and Alistair Blair were already tried and tested, as too was Philippa MacKinnon, a former flat-mate of the Princess of Wales, who had first been introduced to Sarah by their mutual friend, Clare Wentworth-Stanley. Philippa is another of the Real Women Sarah so admires. The daughter of a Yorkshire landowner, she was schooled in Switzerland before deciding to travel the world. While she shared a flat with Lady Diana Spencer she worked at a series of menial jobs to earn the money to travel. During a tour of the Far East she visited a store making and selling dresses in silk. She realized there was no equivalent in Britain and so, aged only twenty-three, coolly borrowed £75,000 from her bank and opened her own shop, the Silk House. Her gamble paid off. Within eighteen months she had paid back the money and established a loyal clientele. Sarah was one, paying £350 a time for the original tailored silk dresses.

She visited Philippa's ground floor apartment just off the Fulham Road for fittings and to bounce around ideas. Sarah prefers strong colors—emerald green and electric blue are particular favorites—and clothes that are tailored rather than loose. Philippa comments, "Sarah has definite ideas. Some clients come in and say they don't really know what they want. But not the Duchess. We would sit down and go through magazines picking out styles and we would also discuss Andrew's ideas. He likes clothes to be neat, tidy, and practical." Like husbands the world over he also wants value for money and is keen that Sarah doesn't buy clothes simply to wear once. Early on Sarah made it clear that she was not entering into a fashion contest with the Princess of Wales, much as fashion editors would have liked to engineer it. She realized she had neither the time, the figure, nor the inclination to compete with her best friend.

As the wedding approached, Sarah brought in other designers to her stable. Suzanne Schneider of Sujon—who made her going-away outfit—was one, Catherine Walker of the Chelsea Design Company was another. Perhaps the most challenging role was given to a former architecture student-turned-designer, Paul Golding. He was commissioned to make the majority of her outfits for Royal Ascot. Everyone knew that Ascot was where the royal romance had started, and it was here that Sarah was determined to make a splash. Golding sketched some of his ideas—"My clothes are unashamedly classic," he argues—and at one of their regular lunches at Claridge's, Sarah showed them to her father. Major Ferguson was startled by the stark bold hoops of one design, disapproving of the childlike milkmaid style of another. His comments were overheard by other diners including ex-King Constantine of Greece. "I thought it looked dreadful and told her so," he recalls. His instinct proved him right. She was roundly criticized for the samurai warrior look which accentuated her curvaceous figure. Even her hairdresser, Denise McAdam, confessed that she too had got her own style wrong that day—"I was trying too hard," she says of the scraped back style. "It aged her. I was also overawed by the 'royal' bit and kept thinking royal, not Sarah." Sarah's discomfiture was not made any easier with the knowledge that Koo Stark, looking chic and demure, was also present in the Royal Enclosure.

So many things to learn, so little time to absorb them. The Princess of Wales was a constant source of help. The Queen too went out of her way to make the royal newcomer feel welcome, and Sarah followed her father's advice—"If you don't know something, don't pretend you do, ask the Queen." Sarah traveled with the Queen to the Easter church service at St. George's Chapel, Windsor and was by her side on the balcony of Buckingham Palace for the celebrations for her sixtieth birthday. It was an emotional occasion as 6,000 youngsters stood in the Palace forecourt waving bunches of daffodils and singing "Happy Birthday." "It looked good from up there," Sarah told reporters who agreed that she had passed her first public appearance with aplomb. Never one to miss an opportunity, she used the Queen's celebration to commission the florist, Jane Packer, to arrange a selection of white and blue lilies for her appearance at the Covent Garden gala. She was so pleased that she summoned Jane to the Palace to discuss the wedding bouquet.

She was similarly aware of opportunities when she joined Princess Margaret to tour the Dulwich Picture Gallery. As she viewed the paintings she was impressed by the efficiency of one young lady. "Are you any good with a word processor?" she asked her. There was a brief interview and by the end Sarah had hired her for a vacant position at the Geneva offices of her publishing company. Her publishing work was never far from her mind, especially her book on the Palace of Westminster. As the author Sir Robin Cooke's condition deteriorated, she brought in the historian Dr. Penny Hunting to help with the research and writing. In the last months Sir Robin was confined to a wheelchair and, with Lady Cooke by his side, would dictate his thoughts into a tape recorder. Sarah was also in regular touch with her employer, Richard Burton, who flew to London each month to monitor the project.

While she found time to make a working visit to the

Grosvenor House Antiques Fair in June, understandably much of her day was taken up with preparations for the wedding. However, many decisions were taken out of her hands. The date for the wedding was chosen by the various private secretaries consulting with the Lord Chamberlain, Lord Airlie, to pick the least disruptive day. Prince Andrew, by contrast, was heavily committed to a six-week officer training course at the Royal Naval College, Greenwich, staying on the base in single officer's accommodations.

Andrew and Sarah originally wanted a honeymoon cruise in the Mediterranean, planning to fly to the south of France to join the royal yacht *Britannia*. However, no one could have anticipated America's bombing raid on Libya. The use of British bases for the mission meant that the yacht, one of the oldest ships in the Royal Navy, would have been a tempting target for Libyan gunboats. Eventually, the royal couple flew to the Azores and had a gentle cruise back to the Solent.

Where Sarah was in command she was firm in her resolve. Early on it was clear that the wedding would produce a small library of books and pamphlets. Some were for profit, others for charity. All wanted to use photographs of her early life. Her new equerry Wing Commander Adam Wise, who had been with Andrew for several years, had severely restricted the number of pictures to be made available. He was a court-ier of the old school who believed all publicity to be a nuisance. He revealed much about his attitude when he was telephoned by a journalist. "Good morning," said the re-porter. Wing Commander Wise replied: "Is it? Even if it was I wouldn't tell you." When Sarah heard that her family pictures were being reviewed she acted swiftly. She rang her father from her office and asked him to make a more compre-hensive selection available.

The books, periodicals, and newspaper articles were just one stream of a torrent of Fergie memorabilia. Within weeks of the engagement you could eat off her, drink from her, smell her, drive her, telephone a sound-alike, book a look-alike, wear her, dry your plates with her and watch her lampooned in the satirical television show, "Spitting Image."

There were even Fergie and Andy garden gnomes for the cogniscenti.

Sarah did the only sensible thing possible—she changed her name. She flew to the Caribbean island of Antigua using the surname Mrs. Watson and stayed with her old school-friend, Florence Belmondo. Unfortunately, it was not long before the world's photographers joined her, and there were further unkind comparisons between the svelte shape of Sarah's friend and her own generous curves. Sarah shrugged it off and treated the press with her usual courtesy and good humor. "I know you've got a job to do," she often said. A diet of local fruits and daily swimming helped her tone up and relax before the very public ordeal to come. As she lay in the shade of a palm tree she could but marvel at the transformation in her life. A year before she was an unknown, a face in the crowd. Now she was on display at Madame Tussauds, her face appeared on postage stamps, and she had her own coat of arms, a bee and a thistle decorated with a bow. (The motifs were originally a crest on some family silver although they neatly symbolized her own industry and Scottish connections.)

Certainly she needed time to relax and calm down. On her public appearances Andrew had had occasion to tell her to shut up because she was getting overexcited. As one friend remarked: "She rattles on about something or someone, asking a lot of questions and can be very interfering. She means well but it can be irritating." However, her bounding enthusiasm was catching. Although a novice on public engagements she showed that she took to the job as though to the manor born. Nor did she mind displaying her affection for Andrew. During a visit to Northern Ireland she put her arm around his neck, and on a tour of an old people's home in Harrogate she gave him a loving cuddle. She was refreshing, totally unstuffy, and appeared to be loving every moment of her new life—and relishing her role to come.

Beneath the banter and bonhomie, here was a couple deeply and sincerely committed to one another. During a meeting at Lambeth Palace with the Archbishop of Canterbury, Dr. Robert Runcie, they discussed the meaning of the wedding ceremony and the obligations and duties of married life. It was Sarah who was behind the decision to use the word "obey" in the marriage service. It properly reflected the conformist, traditional side to her nature. "I'm a great believer that at one stage in a development or a problem somebody has to make a decision," she insists. "I think it's the man's role to be the leader, and therefore he will make the final decision. But that doesn't mean that I'm a 'yes' woman. I must stress that."

A more intractable decision was whether to allow a robot television camera to film the couple in the Abbey as they took their vows. Sarah was happy to let the world share in their spiritual act of union. After all, she argued, weren't the cameras watching everything else? Others including Andrew, were less sure. Unsurprisingly, Sarah, and television companies won the day for this historic royal first. Her father said simply, "Sarah wanted to share her day with everyone. She is a great girl for making everybody happy."

However, the cameras were not on hand to capture the moment when Sarah took off her shoes and played a tune on the organ in Westminster Abbey during one of the rehearsals. She also pinned a 17½-foot train round her waist as the four pageboys and four bridesmaids practiced walking down the aisle behind her. Sarah told them, "We're going to play a game called Grandma's Footsteps, do you know it?" Predictably Prince William stood on the train, and his mother the Princess of Wales voiced her worries to Abbey officials: "I hope he doesn't start tugging the bridesmaids' hair." As a final precaution she took several toy soldiers in her handbag in case William ran amok during the actual service. The rehearsal showed Sarah to be the one who was in command. While Andrew stood on the sidelines it was Sarah who organized the attendants and chatted through the final details with the Dean of Westminster, the Very Reverend Michael Mann.

Under the circumstances the normal high spirits to ease the tension were understandable. Just a few hours before

Sarah and the Princess of Wales had put into effect a plot to invade Prince Andrew's stag night. The comedienne Pamela Stephenson was asked to use her show business connections to rent policewomen's outfits. The unlikely trio planned to raid Andrew's party held at the Camden Hill home of his distant cousin, Richard Lascelles, where guests included Prince Charles, the Scottish comedian Billy Connolly, Elton John and an assortment of naval colleagues. However, Sarah's "lookout," her friend Julia Dodd-Noble, warned the uniformed gate-crashers that press photographers had discovered the venue and were waiting outside. Instead, they went to the exclusive nightclub, Annabels, in Berkeley Square. Once again Julia, wearing "plain clothes," went inside to see if the coast was clear. Inside the club there was another celebration, this time in honor of the *Daily Mail*'s long-serving sports writer, Ian Wooldridge. They took little notice of the three uniformed women who sat demurely drinking orange juice. Finally, one monocled newspaper executive approached the Princess of Wales and, peering at her through his eyepiece, asked if she was a kissogram girl.

They beat a hasty retreat but not before "P.C. Fergie" had had the last laugh on her fiancé. As Andrew's Jaguar swept into a side gate at the Palace the girls, with the connivance of the Royal Protection Squad, stopped his vehicle. They told him that no matter who he was he was not allowed admittance to the Palace so late at night. While he sputtered protestations the girls warned him in the best police clichés that he might have to accompany them to the station and have his particulars taken down. He quickly saw through the ruse as the girls revealed their true identities. The end of the charade came as a relief to the Princess of Wales who complained that her black wig made her feel "hot and uncomfortable" and that her shoes were two sizes too small. She later explained, "The problem was that I didn't really look authentic because the outfit was obviously made for a smaller lady." As for the prank itself she argued, "It did cause a stir but you have to laugh sometimes." Society's sterner spirits felt that the girls were technically breaking the law—impersonating a police officer is an offense—and that it was not proper behavior from the future Queen. Ultimately the waves of enthusiasm before the wedding drowned such criticisms, although they resurfaced when the tide of euphoria ebbed.

During her final weekend as a commoner, that enthusiasm was in full flow when she and Prince Andrew were guests of honor at the Dummer church fête. It was a typical gesture to think of her friends and family. Throughout her engagement Sarah managed to preserve a cheerful perspective toward the mounting hysteria, spending time with those dearest to her heart. She was godmother to Jane's longed-for baby girl, Ayesha, named after the Maharani of Jaipur, whom the girls visited as children, and she was the principal guest at the wedding of her former flatmate, Carolyn Beckwith-Smith. Sarah also found time to maintain her links with Paddy McNally in Switzerland and to write to his sons, Sean and Rollo, at school.

One of the more poignant moments of the wedding week was when Sarah led Paddy by the arm and introduced him to Prince Andrew at a lavish ball thrown by Major Ferguson at the Guards Polo Club. "I've heard all about you," Andrew remarked as they chatted for a short time pausing to watch America's First Lady, Nancy Reagan, take to the dance floor with Prince Philip. The Queen, handbag on her arm, danced with Hector Barrantes, underlining the fact that there was no ill feeling toward the Argentinian polo player in spite of the Falklands conflict.

With the raucous disco music still ringing in her ears, Sarah left the party in the early hours of the morning for her temporary home, Clarence House, the Queen Mother's London residence. While she quietly prepared for her big day, a stream of wedding guests called at Buckingham Palace to deliver their wedding gifts. Her former boss, William Drummond, discovered to his chagrin that his present of a framed picture had to be x-rayed before it was accepted, such was the security surrounding the event.

Like Prince Charles and Lady Diana Spencer before them

A wind-blown Duchess arriving at Weymouth Pavilion for her first public engagement. This is photographer Glenn Harvey's favorite picture. "She looked very glamorous and confident—I feel it captures something of the spirit of Sarah," he says.

The first formal photograph of Princess Beatrice Mary Elizabeth of York taken by her father, the Duke of York, in the drawing room at Balmoral. He used a mirror so that he could see the expression on his daughter's face before using a remote control switch to capture the scene on film. "It was my own idea," he said later.

The Duchess of York, looking very dignified in her diamond tiara and Yves St. Laurent evening gown, poses with the stars of the Broadway production of *Phantom of the Opera*. Actor Michael Crawford, producer Andrew Lloyd Webber, and his actress wife, Sarah Brightman, were hailed for their achievement by normally highly critical New York theater goers.

PHOTO COURTESY LIONEL CHERRUAULT, LONDON

The Duchess courts endless controversy over her wardrobe. Her choice of a leather skirt for an exhibition of Russian Court dress at the Barbican in London provoked criticism—even from her father, Major Ronald Ferguson. "I didn't think it was appropriate," he complained.

"Check out the hair, boys," was the Duchess's comment to waiting photographers when she arrived at an engagement sporting the flags of Britain and America in her hair.

PHOTO COURTESY TIM GRAHAM, LONDON

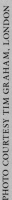

PHOTO COURTESY TIM GRAHAM, LONDON

The Duchess's first official tour of Australia was dogged by controversy. Her decision to leave baby Princess Beatrice at home and then spend a month following Andrew's ship, HMS *Edinburgh*, around the Australian coast did not win universal public approval.

PHOTO COURTESY LIONEL CHERRUAULT, LONDON

The Duchess was quite at home among the cowboys and cowgirls when she was the guest of honor at the Medicine Hat Stampede during her Canadian tour in 1987.

The Duchess watches her husband as he prepares to fly off the deck of the giant aircraft carrier, USS *Nimitz*. Their tour of the ship was one of the highlights of their Los Angeles trip in 1988, made shortly after the announcement that the Duchess was expecting their first child.

PHOTO COURTESY CAMERA PRESS LIMITED, LONDON

The wedding group photographed by American fashion photographer, Albert Watson. He used a brass cycle horn to bring his royal subjects to attention.

Front row, seated, left to right: the Earl of Ulster, Lady Davina Windsor, Lady Rose Windsor, Andrew Ferguson, Lady Rosanagh Innes-Ker, Zara Phillips, Prince William of Wales, Laura Fellowes, Seamus Makim, Alice Ferguson, Peter Phillips, Lady Gabriella Windsor, Lord Frederick Windsor.

Second Row: Lady Sarah Armstrong-Jones, Princess Margaret, Princess Anne, the Princess of Wales holding Prince Harry, Queen Elizabeth, the Queen Mother, the Queen, the bride and groom, Major Ronald Ferguson, Prince Edward, Mrs. Susan Barrantes, Lady Elmhirst, Mrs. Jane Makim. Behind: the Hon. Mrs. Doreen Wright, Major Bryan Wright, Alexander Makim.

Third row: Viscount Linley, Captain Mark Phillips, Marina Ogilvy, the Prince of Wales, Princess Alexandra, the Duke of Edinburgh, Princess Michael of Kent, Princess Alice, the Duchess of Gloucester, the Duchess of Kent, Lady Helen Windsor.

Back row: James Ogilvy, Prince Michael of Kent, the Hon. Angus Ogilvy, the Duke of Gloucester, the Duke of Kent, and the Earl of St. Andrews.

the royal couple issued a wedding gift list for the 1,800 guests. Their requests were mainly available from the General Trading Company, Asprey's the jewelers, interior designer Charles Hammond, with Thomas Goode supplying the glass and china. The list showed their traditional tastes—Coalport china, Georgian mahogany dining room furniture, solid calico-covered sofas—as well as their sense of fun. A teddy teapot and mugs, pictures of Beatrix Potter animals, ashtrays decorated with butterflies and bugs, and matching tankards initialed "A" and "S" were some of the more modest present ideas.

That night Sarah had a present of her own for the world— a robust television interview which showed an energetic couple deeply and happily in love. Much was made of the repartee between the couple as they sat on a wall at Andrew's base in Portland, Dorset, as well as the evident delight they took in each other's company. They seemed far more relaxed and confident than during their first joint television performance on their engagement day. Sarah caused more than a few raised eyebrows when she discussed the debate surrounding her figure, "A woman should have a trim waist, a good up-top, and enough down the bottom—but not too big," she argues. "A good womanly figure." She was equally frank about her royal role admitting that she would have to "polish up a bit." "I'll have to think slightly more, but I will not change when I go out. I'm just going to be me."

As for the future, she gave an indication of her determination to make her royal married life work by announcing that she wanted to learn to fly so that she could talk about Andrew's navy job—"I want to be able to sit down at dinner and discuss what he's done in the day. It's important for me to know how to fly so I can do that." Her pledge came as no surprise to her friends who had seen her adapt to Paddy McNally's world of motor racing and Kim Smith-Bingham's ski salesmanship.

Significantly too, Sarah emphasized that her life as a commoner would help in identifying with people, particu-

larly young people in her new royal role. "I know about going
for a job and an interview," she said. "I never had my own
flat, always rented rooms and know all the pitfalls."

On her last night as a commoner Sarah watched her own
performance on television as she picked at a cold supper.
Appropriately, her last visitor before she went to bed was the
Princess of Wales who had made the fairytale a reality. As
they talked, the man who had guided Sarah through the
traumas of her life, Major Ferguson, strolled by Clarence
House with his family, chatting to enthusiastic and noisy
well-wishers who were camping in the Mall. The scene was
set for a day to remember. What with the chatter of the
crowd, the early morning tunes from the Highland piper
beneath her bedroom window and her natural pre-wedding
nerves, Sarah did not get much rest.

A peep behind the curtains revealed a slate gray day, cool
but dry. As she sipped a welcome cup of coffee, she distract-
edly watched the early morning television coverage. The
cameras focused on the thousands of well-wishers who had
camped overnight along the route from Buckingham Palace
to Westminster Abbey, the teams of armed police who
guarded every rooftop and the Household Cavalry who had
been up before down to polish their silver buckles and breast-
plates.

Before long Sarah's own rooms were a hive of activity as
first her hairdresser, Denise McAdam, and then Lindka
Cierach arrived to prepare the bride. Denise had already seen
the finished dress and had several practice sessions to fix
Sarah's elaborate Edwardian-style floral headdress. While
manicurist Beverly Nathan cared for the bride's nails, beauti-
cian Teresa Fairminer applied a light dusting of make up and
green eye shadow. A telephone call from Andrew, who wore
the full ceremonial dress of a naval lieutenant, brought a little
light relief as the tension built up. Finally, the months of
planning and endeavor came together as Lindka helped
Sarah into her dress, a creation that had started as a few
pencil marks on a page, grown into a cloth toile and now was
about to be displayed to the world.

Meanwhile, as Prince Andrew and his supporter Prince Edward clattered by Clarence House on their way to the Abbey, Major Ferguson, wearing his father's morning coat, nibbled a ginger biscuit, sipped a cup of coffee, and coolly passed the time of day with the Queen Mother's equerry as he waited for his daughter. He also made sure that the eight bridesmaids and pageboys were behaving themselves. Their outfits reflected the theme that Sarah wanted to emphasize— Andrew's navy life and her ancestry. Princess Anne's son, Peter Phillips, and Sarah's half-brother, Andrew Ferguson, wore seventeenth-century midshipman dress uniforms, while the youngest pageboys, Prince William and Sarah's nephew, Seamus Makim, were dressed in Victorian sailor suits. As a delightful finishing touch both midshipmen received a 1758 silver sixpence and both sailors were given an 1846 silver groat in recompense for their pains. Indeed, the midshipmen did suffer for Sarah's artifice for when they sat crosslegged for the photo session in Buckingham Palace they complained bitterly that their leggings cut into them. As for the brides-maids—Princess Anne's daughter Zara Phillips, Lady Rosanagh Innes-Ker, the eldest child of the Duke and Duchess of Roxburghe, Laura Fellowes, the eldest daughter of the Queen's deputy private secretary, Robert Fellowes and the Princess of Wales's sister, and Alice Ferguson, Sarah's half-sister—they looked delightful in their peach dresses which also had the bee, bow, and thistle motif threaded through them. The attendants were whisked quietly to the Abbey as the Queen Mother and Sarah finished dressing.

Upstairs Sarah still couldn't believe the image that faced her in the mirror. "Is this really me?" she asked Lindka. It was a question her father was to ask in a different form minutes later. As she walked down the carpeted stairway he recalls his reaction. "It was the most extraordinary vision," he said. "I was absolutely bowled over. At that moment I was prepared for anything. Stupid jokes to relax her and so on. But as soon as I looked at her face I knew there was no necessity whatsoever to go into any charades to calm her down. There was a serene happiness to her. She was completely relaxed. At the bottom of the steps one of the attendant dressmakers trod on her train, and Sarah let out the usual sort of expletive. I knew then we were in business."

Just forty-eight hours before the wedding Sarah had called her father on his car phone as he was driving down the motorway and told him that come what may she was going to enjoy her wedding day. She was true to her word. As they left Clarence House in the Glass Coach, her face broke into a huge smile the moment she and her father appeared before the cheering crowds. As a commoner Sarah should have only had a police escort along the route. However, because of her family's long regimental association, she was allowed an escort of Life Guards. While they were progressing along the wedding route, Lindka jumped into a waiting black limousine and sped to the entrance of the Abbey to await Sarah. The chorus of the "Grand Young Duke of York" with which the crowd greeted Prince Andrew had barely died away before Sarah made her dramatic appearance at the great West Door. All eyes were on the dress as Lindka and an assistant organized the train—with a helping hand from the bride's father. As the crowd cheered its acclaim, Sarah's boast that "There will never be another dress like it," was amply justified. Then to a rousing fanfare from the Royal Marines and the sound of Elgar's "Imperial March," the bridal party began the slow walk down the blue-carpeted aisle. "Do you know the way?" Sarah joked to her father. "I'm following the blue," he replied. As they made their stately progress Sarah seemed unruffled that the eyes of eight hundred million people were upon her. She was more concerned that she could not smell the scent of the white and pink-peach Jack Frost roses with which the National Association of Flower Arrangers had spent two days decorating the Abbey.

Behind her the attendants behaved impeccably, holding hands and careful not to stand on her train, which exactly fitted the width of the aisle. (This was another triumph of attention to detail. Lindka had measured it before starting work.) Nevertheless, Prince William's concentration was sorely tested during the service as he toyed with his miniature sailor's knife and pulled faces at the other attendants. "It was very hot in the Abbey. He did very well," said the Princess of Wales with some relief afterwards.

Sarah, too, breathed a sigh of relief as she reached the Sacrarium steps without a hitch. She greeted Andrew with a broad smile as he looked with obvious admiration at her dress. Then she carefully negotiated the steps towards the altar before giving her bouquet to her eldest bridesmaid, Lady Rosanagh. The young couple stood quietly and thoughtfully before the Archbishop of Canterbury, Dr. Robert Runcie, as the service began. Typically, the tone was solidly traditional, the couple deciding to follow the liturgy of the 1662 Book of Common Prayer. When Sarah made her promise to obey she gave a quick sideways glance to Andrew and smiled as she said, "I give thee my troth." Before the ceremony she practiced the pneumonic ACE to ensure she got his Christian names in the correct order. However, as she went through the litany of Andrew Albert Christian Edward she stumbled over Christian and quickly repeated it. When the Archbishop asked, "Who giveth this woman to be married to this man?" Major Ferguson firmly presented his daughter's left hand to Dr. Runcie. However, the Book of Common Prayer demands the right hand, an ecumenical error that produced a whimsical *Times* editorial on the subject.

No matter. At least Prince Edward had remembered the ring of Welsh gold that Prince Andrew placed on the fourth finger of Sarah's left hand. There was a ripple of surprise in the congregation as she in turn produced a gold band for Andrew. The couple knelt as Dr. Runcie joined their right hands together and pronounced them man and wife. Sarah Margaret Ferguson was now Her Royal Highness, the Duchess of York, Countess of Inverness and Baroness Killyleagh. The Queen had granted Prince Andrew those titles earlier that morning, the Irish town of Killyleagh being the County Down home of Sarah's ancestors.

It was a gesture expected and in keeping with the wholly conventional nature of the service. Westminster Abbey itself was a return to royal tradition following the choice of St. Paul's by Prince Charles. The last Duchess of York, the Queen Mother, was married there as too were the Queen, Princess Margaret, Princess Alexandra, and the Princess Royal. Hymns, including "Come down O Love Divine" and "Lead us Heavenly Father, Lead Us," were as familiar as the music, which included William Walton's "Crown Imperial" and Handel's "Music for the Royal Fireworks," was rousing.

As the newly created Duke and Duchess of York were signing the wedding register, two vaulting motets by Mozart were sung by the American Arlene Auger and the world renowned soprano Felicity Lott. The mood of serious purpose changed to that of family affection when the royal couple returned hand in hand to the Sanctuary. The Duchess had replaced her floral headdress with a diamond tiara borrowed from a friend and thrown back the veil from her face. While the Duke doffed a smart neck bow towards the Queen, the Duchess dropped a deep curtsey as an expression of her joy. "It was my proudest moment," recalls Major Ferguson. As the couple walked down the aisle, Sarah gave her friend Carolyn Cotterell a stage wink and smiled at her former employers, her friends, and her old boyfriends. Paddy McNally and Kim Smith-Bingham were there as were Lulu Blacker, Laura Geodhuis, Philippa MacKinnon, and Clare Wentworth-Stanley. They had witnessed her heartaches and her disappointments. Now they saw her at her moment of pure happiness and triumph. It was an emotional progress, shared by the crowds and echoed by the pealing of the Abbey's ten bells.

The royal couple traveled in the 1902 State Landau, replete with a Good Luck silver horseshoe on the seat. Behind them were two liveried footmen, one an armed Royal Protection Officer. Following the royal couple were the Queen and Major Ferguson who looked rather restrained and in a third carriage Prince Philip and Susie Barrantes who seemed to enjoy the affair enormously. So did the attendants who hugged and kissed the couple as they arrived at Buckingham Palace.

The 120 guests at the Palace who shared in the wedding breakfast of salmon, lamb, strawberries and cream, together with vintage Bollinger champagne applauded when the Duke and Duchess cut the five-tiered wedding cake, with the Duke's ceremonial sword. The cake, made by the Royal Naval Supply School at *HMS Raleigh* in Cornwall, had as a part of its decorations a polo player, the mythical figure of Pegasus and Van Gogh's "Sunflowers" which were chosen specifically by the Duchess. Outside the Palace the Nikon choir of photographers waited to serenade the royal couple when they made their obligatory balcony appearance. Meanwhile, the official photographer, Scots-born Albert Foster, was having trouble getting his royal charges to assemble in the Throne Room. While the Duke and his photographer mentor, Gene Nocon, tried to help the increasingly flustered cameramen, the rest of the two families paid no attention. Foster recalls, "I realized there was no sign of the Queen. When I looked around she was being helped up a ladder by my assistant so she could look through the camera itself." The other royals followed her lead, while the bridesmaids and pages bowled their floral hoops up and down the Queen's gallery. He used a trick he once pulled when photographing a group of fifty rowdy American stuntmen. He took out a brass cycle horn and with a few fruity toots brought them to attention.

No sooner had he finished then they were once more oblivious to the waiting crowds and the expectant cameras. Sarah seized the respite from formality to snatch a brief chat with Diana, who then, with Prince Harry cradled on her hip, joined the Duke and Duchess on the balcony no doubt recalling her own wedding day five years before. As the crowds yelled "Give her a kiss," the Duke and Duchess put their hands to their ears as if to say, "We can't hear you." Finally the Duke obliged.

The Duchess changed into her flowery Suzanne Schneider going-away outfit before climbing into the carriage waiting to take her to Chelsea Hospital. The Queen and Princess Margaret led the well-wishers who waved them off from the Palace forecourt. Prince William was restrained by his grandmother when he tried to run after the carriage—perhaps he wanted a second look at the giant teddy bear installed there by the Princess of Wales and Viscount Linley. At the back there was a model satellite dish and a message saying "Phone Home," a reference to Major Ferguson's complaint that the Duchess would never call him now that she was a member of the royal family. In fact, she rang him twice from the royal yacht *Britannia* during her honeymoon but on both occasions he was out. At the Hospital, home of the Chelsea Pensioners, the new Duchess chatted to officials and shook hands with the cheerful red-coated occupants. A short helicopter flight then took them to Heathrow and their British Aerospace 146 jet and a honeymoon in the Azores on board *Britannia*.

A day of happiness, a day of excitement, a day when history was made. Sarah had awakened a commoner, she slept a Duchess. The fairy tale had come true.

6
Duchess of York

The booming, bearded figure of King George V cut an imposing swathe through royal drawing rooms and instilled terror into the hearts of his elder sons. He was a naval martinet with a bluff quarterdeck manner who would brook no opposition. At mealtimes he erupted in fury if the Princes were even seconds late. At the other end of the table Queen Mary was a chilling, formidable women whose stern, imperious ways inspired neither affection nor confidences. It is little wonder that Bertie, the Duke of York, was a shy stammerer, that George, Duke of Kent, took to drugs, that Henry, Duke of Gloucester, drank heavily and that Edward, Prince of Wales, quickly found the burden of monarchy too great to bear without the support of the woman he loved, Wallis Simpson.

One begins to realize why Lady Elizabeth Bowes-Lyon, coming from a loving and secure background, had serious doubts about joining such an unhappy family. Yet join it she did, becoming the cornerstone of the House of Windsor in the dark days of the abdication crisis and the Second World

War. She was an immediate success within the family and even George V's thunder was stilled by her charm and cheerfulness. A notoriously poor timekeeper, the new Duchess arrived for dinner late one evening and the King said graciously, "You are not late my dear, I think we must have sat down two minutes early."

Her warmth broke the ice at Court and her wisdom helped guide the family through a turbulent century. Now in her eighties, the Queen Mother, dressed in her familiar blue chiffon, exudes stability and continuity in an unsettled world.

She has been undoubtedly the most influential Duchess of York since the creation of the title in 1385 when Edmund, the fourth son of Edward III was made the first Duke of York. Since then there have been fourteen Dukes, including Prince Andrew, although not all have married. Almost without exception their marriages were concluded for reasons of State and the continuance of the dynasty. Edmund, for example, married Isabel, the daughter of the Portuguese King Pedro I, in order to cement relations between the two countries. During the Wars of the Roses, the white rose of York produced King Edward IV and ill-fated Edward V who, with his young brother Richard, fourth Duke of York, were locked in the Tower of London and there, according to legend and Shakespeare, killed on the orders of their uncle, Richard III.

Richard III himself was killed on the field of Bosworth where Henry VII became the first Tudor King. Henry married Edward IV's daughter, Elizabeth, and so grafted together the white rose of York and the red rose of Lancaster, creating their second son Duke of York, who succeeded to the throne as Henry VIII.

During the seventeenth century, James II's two Duchesses of York bore him the grand total of thirteen children. His first wife, Anne Hyde, was mother to the future Queen Mary II and Queen Anne, while his second wife, Mary of Modena, was the mother of James Edward Stuart, whose family of Pretenders to the English throne was to plague the monarchy for many years to come with threats of a Stuart revival.

In the eighteenth century the title is best remembered for inspiring the nursery rhyme, "The Grand Old Duke of York." The then Duke of York, Frederick Augustus, marched ten thousand troops to the top of a hill and marched them down again. Though a conscientious Field Marshal, he led the British Army to the Netherlands where, after a disastrous campaign against an elusive French Army, he returned home in disgrace. At Court his very public and notorious affair with the Duchess of Rutland did not seem to worry Federick's Duchess, Princess Frederica of Prussia. She busied herself with her garden and her dogs—she had over fifty of them and buried them in their own graveyard at her home in Surrey.

By contrast the last two Duchesses of York have been models of domestic propriety and fidelity. Yet Princess Victoria Mary, daughter of Prince Francis of Teck, would never have become the Duchess of York, later Queen Mary, if her first fiancé, Prince "Eddy," the eldest of Queen Victoria's grandsons, had not died within a few weeks of the announcement of their engagement. A weak-willed and wayward young man, he is probably best known as the most memorable suspect in the long search for the identity of the notorious Victorian murderer, Jack the Ripper. His younger brother, George, was, with almost indecent haste, substituted by Queen Victoria as bridegroom.

This Duchess of York was shy, easily embarrassed, disgusted at the very process of carrying and bearing children and was a forlornly cold and distant wife and mother, able to show her affection only in letters and notes. She rejoiced in State ceremonials, had a magpie's acquisitiveness for both jewelry—"Granny's chips" as the present Queen calls them—and other people's *objets d'art*. She was puritanical in her austere sense of destiny and duty. "You are a member of the British Royal Family. We are never tired and we all love hospitals," she once told a complaining younger member during a visit to the war wounded.

Queen Mary cultivated the mythology of royal distance and was aghast when Lady Elizabeth Bowes-Lyon gave an interview to a newspaper shortly before her engagement, and also when, as Duchess of York, she engineered a series of little volumes about her joyous life with the Duke and their two children, Princess Elizabeth and Princess Margaret. Perhaps the best known was Lady Cynthia Asquith's *The Married Life of HRH the Duchess of York*, written, said the author proudly, with the *personal approval* of Her Royal Highness. The Duchess was determined to make everyone aware that she was the royal embodiment of maternal virtue and skillfully used the media to project an image of an ordinary and happy life. Her love affair with the camera has continued to this day. On a recent tour of Canada she wandered down a race-track waving to nonexistent crowds knowing that television cameras were there to film her.

It is an awareness shared by the present Duchess. "How is it going, everything OK?" she will ask cameramen on a royal tour and is eager to ensure that they get their shots. Scottish photographer Ken Lennox, who has been taking pictures of the Queen Mother for twenty years, says, "The similarities are uncanny. They both have that instinct of knowing exactly where the cameras are and never fail to try and give the boys a decent picture. No matter what has been written about her, the Duchess always keeps her head up and keeps smiling. A real professional."

In many other ways the similarities between these two women, separated by generations yet united by a single title, are quite remarkable. Neither was born to the purple yet both were immediately popular within the royal family. The comments of Queen Mary on Bertie's wife, "Elizabeth is perfectly charming, so well brought up, a great addition to the family," could well apply to the present Duchess. "Such a sensible girl," the Queen tells her friends as she speaks proudly of Sarah's exploits as a helicopter pilot and canoeist. Indeed, such is her affection that she frequently refers to her as "my daughter." Prince Philip has been completely won over by her willingness to join in. "They like her because she has been the one who has tried," says a close friend. "She doesn't need to compromise herself because making an effort

with other people has always been part of her personality."
She has tried carriage driving at Sandringham with Prince
Philip and often joins the Queen on her morning rides. The
Duchess traveled to Cambridge especially to see Prince
Edward appear in a stage revue, and she has discussed the
plans for her home with architecturally minded Prince
Charles. She is at home with the royal family's boisterous
competitiveness and playful pranks from which no one is
immune. The family still talk about the time at Balmoral
when Prince Andrew put armfuls of thistles in Prince
Charles's bed and when Princess Anne hung plastic spiders
in the room of her insect-hating maid. During a Christmas
dinner at Windsor Castle the Queen Mother was hit in the
eye by a ball of brandy butter flicked by Prince Charles.
Typically she wiped it from her eyes and carried on chatting
as though nothing had occurred. The verbal jousting within
the royal family is meat and drink to the Duchess.

The Queen Mother and the Duchess both thrive on the
company of others, enjoying the buzz of conversation, the
banter, and the bonhomie. In their own ways both managed
to shock the Court, the Queen Mother by allowing the Press
access to so many deliciously trivial and sugary facts about
her daughters, the present Duchess for her determination to
continue working and her overfamiliarity with the media.
Their aim, too, has been similar—to promote the image of
happily married couples. The present Duchess's insistence to
the point of tiresomeness that Prince Andrew prefaces every
public utterance with the word "we" rather than "I," is an apt
illustration of this remorseless togetherness. However, both
women have found a peace and an inner strength through the
institution of marriage. And beneath the polite chit-chat
lurks a thread of steel and a calm resolve. In the Duchess's
eyes one can occasionally discern a flinty sense of purpose, an
awareness of the sacredness of monarchy that would have
found resounding affirmation with Queen Mary. As one
friend said wryly, "In twenty years time I can see Fergie as a
sort of diesel-powered dowager Duchess, her children sailing
in her formidable wake, and the kind of ample bosom one

could serve a tray of drinks from. Yes, royal life will suit her
well. She will grow into the job."

Her first real taste of the privileges and pleasures of royal
life came the day after her wedding when she lazed on board
the highly polished deck of the royal yacht *Britannia* as it
cruised elusively around the islands of the Azores. For the
first time in months she had the chance to relax away from
the cameras and spend some time alone with her husband.
Alone that is except for 276 officers and ship's company
who padded noiselessly around the Queen's floating palace.
They slept in a double bed—normally stowed in the hold—
in the Queen's rooms, watched videos of the wedding specially flown to the yacht, listened to their favorite Elton John
and Chris de Burgh tapes, chatted to the men and invited
a handful of officers to join them for dinner. Each morning
they planned their day's sailing, musing over charts with
the yacht's captain, Rear Admiral Sir John Garniere, in the
glassed-in veranda deck. They went water skiing, swimming, enjoyed barbecues on solitary beaches, and watched
some of the sailors fishing for tuna from the foredeck. In the
afternoons they conscientiously answered the many thousands of goodwill messages and sent handwritten notes to
their friends thanking them for their wedding presents.
Often these were accompanied by a signed wedding photograph now adorning many a drawing room in Pimlico,
Fulham, and Battersea. The Duke took Sarah on a guided
tour of the yacht, joking about the history behind the so-
called "Golden Rivet" in the yacht's spotless engine room.
The phrase, which has various salty connotations, was regularly used by Victorian seafarers when they wanted a little
privacy with their loved ones. However, when a youthful
Prince Charles asked the yacht's captain to see the legendary
"Golden Rivet," it was felt that he was too young to be told
about life below deck. Instead one of the rivets in the white
engine room was indeed painted gold and remains so to this
day.

At the end of the voyage a concert was organized by the
ship's company for the entertainment of the royal couple.

There were jokes about helicopters, bees (and birds), and the pretensions of the Supergirl who wanted to learn to fly. These concerts are a regular ritual as too is the cat-and-mouse game between the world's press and *Britannia*. On every royal honeymoon—those of Princess Margaret, Princess Anne, and Prince Charles—the media have tried and failed to harpoon the yacht with their long distance lenses. This voyage was no different despite one intrepid reporter who hired an island ferry to search for *Britannia*.

The honeymoon was not without its mishaps. As the rest of the royal family joined the yacht for the traditional cruise around the Western Isles of Scotland, the Duchess badly injured her left knee in a water skiing accident. Indeed the Duchess admits that she seems prone to mishaps—the car that wouldn't start when she returned from Klosters, the gun that jerked back in her eye during a stag shoot, the royal Rolls-Royce that broke down on the way into Los Angeles, the helicopter that had to make a forced landing when flying the Duchess to see Niagara Falls, the steel rope that whistled past her face as she waved at the Duke's frigate in Perth, Australia, and the chauffeur who drove into a police escort car during her first tour abroad to the Netherlands. As one friend recalls, "If ever a dress tore it was Fergie's, and it was always her tights that ran at an embarrassing moment." Some of her more superstitious friends felt the Duchess was tempting fate by skiing during her pregnancy.

When she arrived back at the Palace from her honeymoon the Duchess's knee was heavily strapped. During her absence her belongings had been moved into Prince Andrew's apartments on the second floor overlooking the Mall and visible to the thousands of sightseers who come in the forlorn hope of catching a glimpse of royalty. The Duke jokes with visitors that he daren't pull back the curtains and look out or else everyone would wave at him. They are unremarkable rooms, decorated by a friend, the interior designer Sophia Stainton. Comfortable rather than palatial, the sitting room is dominated by a huge squashy sofa, Andrew's own photographs and the occasional period painting on loan from the Queen's extensive collection. In one corner is a well-stocked drinks cabinet. The Duke, a Coca-Cola only man, serves stiff measures as is the wont of teetotalers. Next to it is a sophisticated stereo system. The Duchess brought along her record collection, mostly middle-of-the-road rock—Elton John, David Bowie, and Phil Collins with a smattering of Beethoven and Mozart—to add to his offerings of Feargal Sharkey, Tina Turner, and Queen. As this was now a home rather than a *pied à terre*, the Yorks acquired several more rooms for the Duchess. She was given her own dressing room and her temporary study, once used by the Duke of Windsor, became a permanent fixture. Down the corridor Prince Edward and Princess Anne had their rooms and offices, while another near neighbor was the legendary figure of Bobo MacDonald, the Queen's dresser who has been by her side for over half a century.

In those first few weeks she saw rather more of her neighbors than she did of her husband. He left for an intensive course at a naval base in Yeovilton, Somerset, to train as a weapons instructor. For him married life revolved around a telephone call to the Palace at the end of the day's lectures followed by an evening's studying in his spartan officer's cabin with only a framed photograph of his wife for company. For the Duchess, life was rather more luxurious, and it took a lot of getting used to. From being called "Miss Ferguson" by Palace staff, she was now addressed as "Your Royal Highness" at first greeting and thereafter as "ma'am." Even her father was taken aback. When she called him at his Dummer home the Palace operator told Major Ferguson, "Will you please hold the line for the Duchess of York?" Nonplussed he replied, "Who?" before the realization dawned upon him. However, she insisted that her close friends call her by her old name—except in public.

One friend recalls, "She arrived for a dinner party soon after her elevation, and no one quite knew whether to stand up, bow, or curtsey, call her Your Royal Highness, or what. Fergie made her feelings plain the moment she walked into the room. She obviously saw the bewildered looks and said straightaway, 'Look you lot, it's Fergie or Sarah, none of this Your Highness nonsense, OK?' The message soon got around." Now her friends initially refer to "the Duchess" in cooing tones, but after a few minutes they soon relax into "Fergie" or "Sarah."

Without warning the Duchess found she had more friends than she had ever dreamed of. They all wanted favors. As one of her genuine friends recalls, "Where you might think of one or two phone calls, read twenty. Everyone had a friend of a friend who had some worthwhile cause they wanted her to support. When she had no one, when Paddy was at his worst, they were the same so-called friends who were being mean and spiteful to her. Now they all wanted to come back into the fold." Her equerry, Wing Commander Adam Wise had one solution—to turn down everyone, making it abundantly clear that the Duchess was not in the business of favoritism. It ruffled a few feathers, especially when true friends had had their invitations accepted verbally by the Duchess only to receive a tart letter turning them down.

While Palace life does confine her, she tries to see her close circle of friends frequently. She rings her father and step-mother virtually every day, and Paddy McNally, too, is often called for advice and a gossip. They occasionally see each other in London but have to be extremely careful. As one friend put it, "The wrong interpretation would be put on a picture of them together, and there would be unnecessary speculation." Her real friends—Carolyn, Laura, Clare, Lulu, and Julia—she sees for lunch, dinner, and weekend parties although naturally not as often as she would like. As one wailed recently, "She is so booked up she can't come for dinner until October."

With her husband away for much of her marriage, the Duchess has thrown herself into her royal duties, her pub-lishing work, and her growing portfolio of charities. Her days start around 6:30 in the morning and end around midnight. Her motto is: "The busier you are the more time you make," a view borne out by her hairdresser, Denise McAdam, who visits her at the Palace every time she has an official engagement. "She is a great rusher," she says. "She's usually got about fifteen minutes, an hour if you're lucky." Other friends testify: "She flies around at a rate of knots, can't keep still for a moment." However, every day begins in a truly civilized, time-honored fashion as a footman brings a quaintly named "calling tray" from the kitchen and leaves it outside her bedroom door beneath a stern oil painting of Queen Mary. A uniformed maid gently raps on the door and carries in the white Minton cup and saucer, milk jug, and pot of Darjeeling tea. While the Duchess dresses, the footman— or the Yorks's valet, Michael Perry—lays the breakfast table. "No, it is not like a high class hotel," sniffs one servant. "Where else could you eat with George III silver cutlery at breakfast?" Strawberry yogurt, croissant (baked in the Palace kitchens), brown toast, and strong Brazilian blend coffee are her usual fare, although she still likes a hearty English breakfast of sausage, bacon, and eggs. During her pregnancy, when she ballooned up from a size 10 to size 14, she did, like many women before her, eat for two.

On a side table the footman lays out the morning papers for her to browse through, while a maid quickly tidies her bedroom. Before breakfast she likes to take the elevator down to the indoor royal pool and join the Princess of Wales—she normally arrives at 7:15—for an early morning swim. Now that she doesn't ride or play tennis as she did, this is her only regular exercise. Occasionally the Princess may join her for breakfast but, even though they are close friends, these days there is no question of simply popping in. Their lives are ruled by printed timetables that state when and where they are going so that everyone from the cook to the private secretary can make their plans. Life is a tyranny of timetables, endless memos, and meetings—"Notes, notes, always notes," says the Duchess as she tries to juggle requests for royal engagements, her publishing activities, and her behind-the-scenes work for her charities, particularly the Search 88 Cancer Trust. Her mornings are spent in her study, answering letters, talking on the telephone, and chairing meetings.

At eleven o'clock there is a break for coffee—but the pace is remorseless.

From the start she displayed her determination to fulfill her vow to Prince Andrew that she would learn to fly. Three afternoons a week she drove herself to RAF Benson, the Oxfordshire home of the Queen's Flight, where she met her flying instructor, Colin Beckwith. He worked for a flying school run by Lord Waterpark, an Old Etonian friend of the Fergusons, who loaned her his chief instructor and a £50,000 Piper Warrior as a wedding present. The Duchess's decision to take to the skies had the full backing of Andrew and Prince Philip who says, "I feel very strongly that flying isn't a sort of black art which can only be done by devotees or daredevils."

They both admire her ferocious enthusiasm to master the arts, to learn about map reading and meteorology in the classroom, and to read about the principles of aviation as "homework." After just twenty-two days of intensive tuition "Chatterbox One"—the nickname air traffic controllers gave the talkative royal—made her first solo flight and was presented with her wings early in 1987. "I am constantly surprised by her, she does everything very well indeed," said the admiring Duke, who was flown by her from RAF Benson to Oxford, where the chairman of the Civil Aviation Authority handed over her license. While she became the first royal female ever to hold a private pilot's license she never forgot her instructor, Colin Beckwith, who took her under his wing. Typically she sent flowers to his daughter, Jenny, when she celebrated her eighth birthday and telephoned Mr. Beckwith when he was forced to leave his job by a new management. "I wasn't surprised that she called, she is that kind of girl," said her instructor who, not surprisingly, had earlier named her as his "Pupil of the Year."

Several months later his faith was confirmed when she had her first chance of aerobatics after watching a nerve-tingling display by the famous Red Arrows flying team. Watched by the Duke, she joined Squadron Leader David Walby in a

Bulldog trainer and took to the skies over the Humber estuary. After he took her through a barrel role and several wingovers, this royal "Top Gun" took the controls herself, flew her first loop the loop, yelling, "I've done it!" over the headset as she eased back in her seat. "She has great courage, nerve, and a lot of character," said Squadron Leader Walby. Since that experience she has now decided that her latest aerial ambition is to fly a jet.

Perhaps her greatest triumph was when she took her father for a spin over his Dummer farm as a Christmas present. As they flew over the rolling countryside they could distinctly make out the herb garden with the initials "A" and "S" intertwined—a wedding gift from her stepmother. "It was the best Christmas present I've ever had," said the Major, recalling that before she became a Duchess she had never even been in a light plane.

Yet she was not content to rest on her laurels. Another wedding gift from Lord Hanson, of the business conglomerate, the Hanson Trust, allowed her to learn to fly helicopters, using one of his private fleet of Jet Ranger choppers. She took just forty-one hours of flying to win her wings—once again the first royal female ever to achieve such a prize. Her husband, a veteran navy helicopter pilot, confessed that it took him twice as long and without the distractions and pressures of royal life. She admitted that the worst moment was making an emergency landing with the engine switched off, but felt her efforts were worthwhile, "I now know exactly what he's talking about when he comes home from a day's flying." The Duchess subsequently put her skills to practical purpose when she arrived for the christening of Charlotte McGowan's daughter, Laura, by helicopter. The royal godmother managed to land perfectly in a field by their Northamptonshire farm.

Noticeable, too, was the way she brought her own inimitable style to this primarily male occupation. Her brown leather flying jacket, the suede boots and trousers, and her specially made bi-plane hair clips reflected the Duchess's personality. It is little wonder that fashion photographer Terry O'Neill specifically chose this Biggle outfit as most representative of her relaxed informal character when he was asked to take the official portraits before her tour of California in 1988.

While her flying has taken up many afternoons, on other days at the Palace she was in her office and allowed herself the indulgence of that royal ritual, afternoon tea. At 4:30 prompt, a footman brings in a tray of tiny cucumber, ham, or cheese sandwiches and the Queen's favorite, a rich dark chocolate cake. However, the Duchess does not have a sweet tooth. "I'm a savory person," she says, relishing quiche, steak and kidney pie, roast chicken, and lamb. Since living at the Palace she has grown tired of smoked salmon and more fussy about what she eats—a habit that annoys the chefs who like order and routine in their lives.

While her nonstop work routine left the staff breathless, it did wonders for her figure, the adrenaline surge helping her to shed more than a stone in weight.

In the evening she often works until nine on her papers, pausing at 8:15 for dinner to be served. It is not lavish— prawn cocktail, steak, raspberries and cream, and a glass of Bordeaux are her regular requirements. At times, especially in the first weeks of marriage, she was lonely with her husband away and her friends inevitably held at arms' length. They can't ring her and ask if she wants to come out for a meal or a drink as they did in the old days. "I'm worried that she might think I'm being pushy, imposing myself," says one. "I now wait for her to call, but of course she has a thousand and one things on her mind,"—views held by a chorus of her friends.

As her father says, "She found it strange having a husband who had to go off almost from the moment they were married, even though she knew what she was in for from the start." It was not the happiest way to settle down to married life. All those tiny trivial decisions that help cement a relationship were passing them by. Telephone calls in the evenings could never compensate for a face-to-face conversation, especially between such an obviously physical couple. Their weekends together were sacred although not without their problems. As she says, "I burn the candles at both ends, get up far too early so my weekends are spent asleep." Nor was the Duchess the only culprit. As she moaned to one friend, "Andrew comes home on Friday absolutely tired out. On Saturday we have a row. On Sunday we make it up but by then he has got to go back to base again."

She looked on with more than a little envy as she saw her old flatmate Carolyn Cotterell happily setting up home in Herefordshire, while her own wedding gifts were gathering dust in the disused Palace cinema. The royal couple had already decided that he should make the Royal Navy a long-term career—he signed on the "general list" in October 1986 indicating his commitment. They knew, too, that he would be posted back to his old base at Portland, Dorset and therefore set about looking for a house that would help solve the problem of their long distance marriage. Prince Andrew enlisted the help of Captain Robert Woodard, an usher at their wedding, and the Lord-Lieutenant of Dorset, Lord Digby, to find a suitable secure property for them to rent.

This proved more difficult than expected. Several houses were examined by Scotland Yard bodyguards and found to be too vulnerable. Another house, owned by an Austrian diplomat, Max Turnauer, was discounted when a national newspaper photographed the interior. "I'm not sleeping where some reporter has been standing in my bedroom!" the Duke is said to have exclaimed. Finally, a firm of estate agents found an appropriate property for the royal couple, Chideock Manor deep in the heart of Thomas Hardy country.

The five-bedroom Regency mansion was owned by Charles Weld, a member of one of the most influential Catholic families in the country. Next door to the stone-built property was the Catholic church of Our Lady, Queen of Martyrs, which was still used in spite of the royal presence. The two-hundred-year-old house boasted a secret passage down to the chalk cliffs a mile away and was reputedly haunted by ghosts from the Civil War. A bleak, rather forbidding place, their choice did not prove a success. The Duchess never felt comfortable renting the isolated manor house, away from her circle of friends with only ghosts for company when Andrew was away on night duty.

"She never felt she could make it her home," says a friend. "It was too remote and inconvenient." Left unsaid was the rather more touchy subject of money. By renting Chideock and paying for the cost of running their apartments at Buckingham Palace they were literally living to the Manor Overdrawn. The Duke's £17,000-a-year naval lieutenant's pay, the Duchess's £15,000-a-year job as a commissioning editor (she had secured a raise shortly after her marriage), together with a Civil List payment of £50,000 (it rose to £86,500 in 1988) scarcely amounted to a king's ransom.

While there will always be dark mutterings about the Civil List, its purpose is to pay for the staff employed by members of the royal family and their incidental expenses, such as day-to-day office costs. Even at Buckingham Palace the Yorks were stretched employing as they did an equerry, a valet, a dresser, a private secretary, a general secretary, together with the expenses of the Duchess's part-time lady-in-waiting, Jocelyn Floyd. Living at the Palace does have its advantages, as the costs of cooks, chauffeurs, housekeepers, and other staff come out of the Queen's pocket. At Chideock they had to employ their own. While Prince Andrew did receive a substantial allowance from the Queen, he and the royal family generally like to make a distinction between public and private costs. For him, the arithmetic of moving to Chideock did not add up.

During their nine-month tenure, they barely visited Chideock Manor for more than three or four weekends even though it was policed around the clock by Dorset police—a fact that caused a few mutterings in the county. They decided to move again when King Hussein of Jordan, closer to the Queen and Prince Charles than many realize, offered to loan the couple his highly secure seven-bedroom home, Castlewood House, on the fringes of Windsor Great Park.

Until then the Duke and Duchess had spent many a weekend staying with friends at their homes in the country. This had also served the purpose of introducing Andrew to the

Duchess's lifelong friends. While Andrew was skeptical, the Duchess was determined to break free from the Palace shackles and lead as normal a life as possible.

On the night of her twenty-seventh birthday, for instance—just one hundred days after their marriage—she arranged a small table at the intimate Waterside Inn restaurant at Bray, a few miles from Windsor. She argued with Andrew that they could behave like an ordinary couple without resorting to endless subterfuge and elaborate precautions. Arriving early with her friend, Carolyn Cotterell, she discovered to her horror that a Fleet Street photographer and reporter were already eyeing the £50 a head menu. She was saddened and rather startled that her plans could be so easily scuppered. When she and Andrew flew to Barbados for a secret holiday at the home of racehorse owner Robert Sangster a few weeks later she was far more careful. "Only eight people in the whole world knew about it," the Princess of Wales gleefully told journalists. "They were determined to have some time alone together." Even at the Sangster's pink villa they were cautious; "Andrew and Fergie couldn't walk along the beach in case they were recognized," said Susan Sangster.

While they had a few friends in common—Clare Wentworth-Stanley was one of Andrew's former girlfriends—the Duke often found himself feeling left out of the conversation as Fergie chattered on about mutual acquaintances with their hosts. At a party in the summer hosted by Susie Barrantes at her Midhurst home he was left silently watching Viscount Linley and the Princess of Wales gymnastically gyrating on the dance floor in the marquee while the rest of his table chatted merrily. One of the party recalls, "Andrew was in a sulk because nobody knew him and so not knowing quite what to do they carried on their conversations across him. He clearly felt ignored. Then Fergie came up kissed him loudly in the ear, ran her hands over his dress shirt and said, 'Cheer up, Andrew,' and took him off for a dance."

They are an obviously physical couple. Many a country house guest has been taken aback by his jolly forays north of the knee as they sit giggling on the sofa. "You're terrible," Andrew says, as she insists on feeding him stringy spaghetti or pizza during simple supper parties with friends.

"Certainly she has loosened up the Duke. He is less stuffy," say friends. In the early days of their marriage there were complaints that he took the efforts of her friends too much for granted. As one recalls, "After all he is a Prince and one is understandably nervous and apprehensive when they come to stay. You do your best to make sure everything is perfect. But he never seemed to notice. Andrew is a lot better now, more thoughtful."

That is not an accusation ever leveled at the Duchess who is sometimes thankful to the point of gushing. She has managed to soften Andrew without too many scenes, having the ability to chastise without bruising the tender male ego. During their first skiing holiday together in Klosters they had an argument as they stood in the mountain train climbing to the slopes. They had been surrounded by photographers and camera crews as they arrived at the station, and the Duchess insisted that she wanted to look her best for the public. She was also concerned for the health of one of the television reporters who had fallen in the snow in front of them.

As they stood in the train Andrew told her, "I don't know why you worry about them." The Duchess, overheard by a magazine journalist traveling in the same compartment, was peeved. "Why do you have to keep embarrassing me and pointing it out in front of other people when I get things wrong? It's not very charitable. Sometimes you're as bad as your father. If you're going to say something like that then why don't you wait until we're on our own instead of embarrassing me? Unlike some people I haven't been doing this for twenty-seven years."

Her blandishments are delivered in a cooing voice, ending with a kiss and a playful pinch of the cheeks. "You are awful but I love you," she says. Then it is on to the next topic as she inspires a lighthearted flow of conversation as energetic as he can be ponderous. She has stopped him from taking himself so seriously. In his bachelor days this royal photographer was rather proud when he discovered a technical error in the Nikon manual. Now he would dismiss this as priggish, and he has learned to change conversational channels when Sarah catches him earnestly buttonholing dinner guests and talking about how it is essential to "keep up to speed" in photography.

For all that they are a couple who are deeply in love, "Oh my God yes, they are happy," says Charlotte McGowan, dismissing the question as a statement of the obvious. She has become more confident, more self-assured, he is less hostile to outsiders—particularly the media—and more reflective and caring. "He is my support, my main right arm," the Duchess says with feeling.

Yet while the Duke is losing that Teutonic stiffness of manner, the Duchess remains more flexible. She learned to fly for him and went canoeing in Canada to please him and even took up photography enthusiastically—although he still takes her official portraits at Balmoral. When he goes salmon fishing or stag hunting, she is dutifully by his side.

Their robust, jesting relationship was nowhere better displayed than with the controversial Royal Knockout Tournament organized by Prince Edward. The event itself epitomized all the uneasy tensions surrounding the royal family during the late twentieth century—commercial sponsorship, unremitting television coverage, and pressure on the royals to behave as clowns one minute, courtiers the next.

Internationally known personalities like rock star Meatloaf, singer Sheena Easton, "Superman" Christopher Reeve, actress Jane Seymour, and former world champion boxer Barry McGuigan were asked by Prince Edward to take part in a day of general nonsense at Alton Towers Leisure Park in the Midlands. The idea was to stage a series of rather juvenile games based on a medieval theme and involving jousting over water and rescuing damsels in distress. The four teams were led by the Duke and Duchess of York, the Princess Royal, and Prince Edward. Their roles were roughly in line with Bagehot's principles of monarchy, to encourage, to consult, and to warn—but not to take part. In this way it was hoped that a dignified distance between the showbiz stars and the royal captains would be maintained. It was not. The devil-may-care tone was set the night before when the royals and the stars sat down together for dinner. Meatloaf paraded round the room with the Duchess on his arm, food was thrown around, and Andrew ended up with most of the contents of a bowl of sugar in his hair—courtesy of his wife.

Although this was little different from other tales of royal high spirits down the years, the hot medium of television brought the high jinks of the Duchess and Duke vividly to life. In her eagerness and inexperience the Duchess forgot that what is acceptable behind closed doors is viewed differently when the spotlight of publicity shines. From the moment the Duchess, dressed in a blue flowing dress, led her team into the arena a mood of enthusiastic mayhem was joined. She led the chant of "Big Bad Blues"—the name of her team—and in a voice hoarse with excitement told the compère Stuart Hall, "We are very bad." As the games progressed and competition between the teams grew keener, she started a food fight with her husband, throwing pieces of plastic fruit that adorned the various banqueting tables. She urged the 250-pound Meatloaf to steal Andrew's panda mascot and stuff it down his trousers, before leading her team in a lap of honor round the muddy field of combat. She resembled not so much a dignified Duchess as the captain of a girls' hockey team who had just beaten their keenest rivals. It was not an edifying spectacle, especially when contrasted with the behavior of the Princess Royal who laughed, joked, and had fun yet still maintained a sense of decorum. The event marked a genuine change in the public's perception of the young royals, a feeling that they were demeaning the dignity of the monarchy.

In her defense it may be argued that the Duchess was merely diving headlong into the lighthearted event with her usual competitive zest. "She does first, thinks later," say friends. Her inexperience led her to forget the presence of the cameras. While commentators asked if the young royals were letting the Queen down, Major Ferguson joined the fray on his daughter's behalf, "She did not go overboard, she was just part of a team and was encouraging them." Certainly television and the press enjoyed a mixed postbag in reaction to the young royals behaving as entertainers. For every reader who complained about their antics, another welcomed their enthusiasm as "wonderfully refreshing" and "full of fun, vigor, and vitality."

People questioned whether Prince Edward should have been allowed to organize the event at all. "Personally I don't think any of the royals should have participated. I don't think that kind of thing is terribly fun," agreed Major Ferguson. he shrewdly put his finger on the endless dilemmas facing the royal family as both fund-raisers for charity and symbols of national life. "We all do things for charity that perhaps we shouldn't do," he explained.

In the debate surrounding the event and the behavior of the young royals much was made of the Queen and how in more than thirty-five years of public life she had never put a foot wrong. "She has set the world an example of conscientiousness and correct behavior," argued gossip writer Compton Miller.

There was tabloid talk of the Queen's "fury," family summits, and Prince Charles reading the riot act to his younger brethren. The truth is more prosaic, but it does cast an intriguing light on the nature of modern royalty and the crucial role of the Duchess of York for the future.

It was George V who inspired the phrase, the "Family Firm," to describe the workings of a modern royalty. This may conjure up images of structure where the Queen acts as chairman of the board, issuing dictates and decrees to the rest of the royal directors who are accountable to the nation of shareholders, a fanciful notion that does not bear close inspection. As one member of the royal family has said, "The royal family is very decentralized. No sensible businessman would allow so much autonomy or allow the organization to run without overall control. We all live in little watertight compartments and you would be amazed at the lack of cooperation between the individual members." At a recent meeting of Lord-Lieutenants—the shire officials behind the organization of royal visits to their counties—one notable complained that they had five visits by different members of the royal family in one week, a total unsurpassed in the previous two decades.

The royal family's plurality of purpose and views is both its strength and weakness. More senior members of the family criticize the Queen for interfering too little in the public lives of her family, while she argues that she feels her children must learn by their own mistakes.

It is very likely an attitude formed during the turbulent mid-1950s. Then, Princess Margaret's life was effectively ruined when the Court and Cabinet decreed that she could not marry the divorced Group Captain Peter Townsend. Since that bitter decision, which with hindsight seems mean and narrow-minded, the Queen has rarely interfered in the lives of her family. The most recent and vivid example was when Prince Edward was allowed to resign from the Royal Marines in the full glare of publicity causing the Services and the family untold damage. Indeed, when historians review the reign of Queen Elizabeth II they will point to a weakness and an overindulgence at the top that allowed an unnecessary degree of drift and damage within the family to occur.

These same historians might also pick out the televised Royal Knockout Tournament as the turning point when the Queen and more conservative members of Court attempted to rein in the younger members of the family. This was how one member of the family explained it. "The family learnt a very nasty lesson, but experiments have got to be made. You will see the tap of publicity being turned off very slowly in the next few years. When a member of the family appears on television we don't sit round discussing it, saying you made an absolute balls of that or whatever. Quite frankly none of them watch television. It isn't discussed. However the Knock-out thing was, and the word has been passed around that 'enough is enough.' " Interestingly, the Duchess has since turned down a proposal from the BBC to make a "fly on the wall" style of documentary about her royal life.

Within Court circles the Duchess of York's antics went largely unremarked. Raised eyebrows certainly, talk about overenthusiasm and inexperience, but in general the Duchess was and is seen as a sound, sensible girl with a strong personality and a profound sense of royal duty and responsibility. She recognized her mistakes, "I must use the gray matter between my ears first," she ruefully told her friends. Indeed, at Court and within the inner circle of royal friends her true value to the Windsors is recognized—that is in helping the Princess of Wales in her role. It is an intriguing relationship.

Nineteen eighty-seven saw the public blooming of a young woman who had been continually defined as shy and demure. While the Duchess is the noisy Labrador of the family, boisterous, loving, but ultimately obedient, the Princess can be described as the Irish Setter, groomed, sleek, skittish, highly strung, and unpredictable. They are extremely close friends—"We have a marvelous relationship," affirms Sarah—but since the Duchess joined the family there have been subtle changes.

The Duchess's arrival within the family circle coincided with Diana's growing independence. She no longer felt intimidated by her royal role and was happy to pass on her own experiences to the Duchess who was eager to learn. Her sons had grown past the difficult stage, and she was in no hurry to have any further children. Diana's relationship with Prince Charles, a constant topic of debate, had settled down to, if not the great love affair of the century, at least a marriage of mutual tolerance and understanding. He went his own way, hosting dinners at Kensington Palace for experts in the fields of architecture, race relations, the environment, and the inner cities, or attending "boy's nights" get-togethers with his older, more worldly friends.

As Sarah's relationship with Andrew developed she was well aware that Diana was beginning to lead her own life. In the early days of her married life, Diana's place in the public spotlight would leave her exhausted and ready for an early night, drained by the constant flow of nervous energy. However, these days she is something of a night owl, visiting West End theaters regularly—she has seen *Phantom of the Opera* three times—and going out to dinner with her own circle of friends who include businessman's daughter Kate Menzies, her old flatmate Caroline Bartholomew, and the Duke of Wellington's daughter-in-law Antonia, Marchioness of Douro.

The most striking feature of Diana's private life is that Charles rarely, if ever, accompanies her. It is a fact of royal life accepted by her circle—"No, it is not natural behavior by a married couple but that is the way it is," says one friend. Their loyalty to the Princess ensures that their comments are circumspect, but the outsider soon appreciates the disapproval they feel over Charles's behavior. "Diana is a very dear person, very sensitive, and one who wants to respect her man," they argue. Her friends had been disconcerted for some time by Charles's habit of leaving country house parties late at night and driving off alone. They became even more alarmed when the Princess herself took to climbing into her Ford Escort car and leaving Kensington Palace on her own. Her assignations, often in the early hours of the morning, were innocent enough—to see friends who live in the Pimlico, Westminster, Belgravia triangle. It was and is her way of escaping from the endless, suffocating claustrophobia of royal life.

On one occasion she arrived at a friend's house wearing just a raincoat over her nightgown. It was after one in the morning, but she wanted a chat, was in a jolly mood, and had known the friend since her schooldays. Unusual, but not eccentric behavior except when one realizes that this is the future Queen.

This well-disguised feature of her life has naturally given rise to concern even among her staunchest allies. "She is taking a hell of a risk. Not just with the publicity but also from a security point of view," said one close girlfriend. "It's highly irresponsible." Others understand her motives, "She has got to let off steam somehow. If the Palace tries to rein her in she will probably do something silly and run off from the whole thing."

It is in this context, with a coltish Princess of Wales champing at the bit of life in the public eye, that the Duchess's true worth to the Court—and the Waleses' marriage—must be assessed. She has become a vital safety valve and has helped ease both the public pressure of publicity and the private problems of Diana's unusual marriage to a man consumed by his own doubts and sense of worth and with a mode of behavior established long before she arrived in his life. Ironically, the Duchess has paid a high price for her friendship, being accused of leading Diana astray and causing her to forget her solemn duty as a future consort. Far from it. Her value has been to expand Diana's circle of friends outside the Palace walls at a time when she was emerging from her social chrysalis and to enable her to fly more freely within the Court instead of beating her wings in frustration against the limitations of royal life. Together they have blown a few of the cobwebs away from the royal rafters, united in their amused ridicule of the "screaming snores," their rhyming slang for the stuffier courtiers who infest the red-carpeted corridors.

Diana's awareness of her own role and power gradually emerged as she grew into the job, and the Duchess provided much welcomed support and encouragement. At the same time the Princess has guided her friend through the labyrinthine workings of the family. They are true friends who gossip together, vie with each other, and confide in each other. Diana has always adopted a wry, rather amused approach to her role, seeing the absurdity in so much of the flummery that attends royal life. Now she has a friend who shares the same jokes.

For the family their first real taste of the new relaxed mood came during the Duchess's first Christmas at Windsor Castle.

Traditionally, the evening of Christmas Day is known as

Brolly good show. The Duchess and the Princess prod their friend Lulu Blacker during a moment of fun at Ascot. Their innocent prank was clouded by a shower of criticism.

The Duchess and beefy rock singer Meatloaf discuss tactics before the Royal Knockout Tournament in the summer of 1987. Four teams of international celebrities including actress Jane Seymour, singer Tom Jones, and boxer Barry McGuigan competed for honors in the games which were set in a mock medieval castle and involved rescuing damsels in distress and jousting over water. The Duke and Duchess of York together with the Princess Royal and Prince Edward, who devised the televised fun day, urged on their teammates as they vied to take first place. While the Tournament raised millions of pounds for charity, it earned many uncharitable comments about members of the royal family taking part in events of this undignified nature.

The Duchess regards, with some concern, a premature baby lying in an incubator in a Cardiff hospital. She made the visit in her role as patron of Action Research for the Crippled Child.

"Fergie Crockett," queen of the wild frontier, paddles away on her Canadian canoeing holiday.

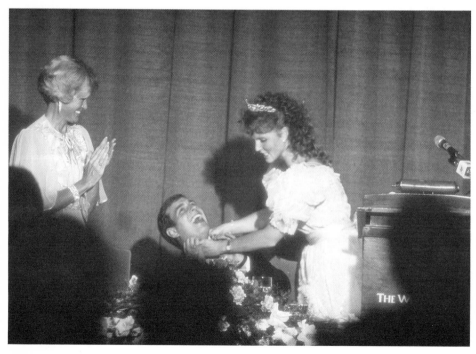

The Duchess warmly shakes her husband by the throat after he made some cheeky remarks during a speech in Edmonton.

An artist's impression of the York's two-story home currently being built within the walled garden of Sunningdale Park near Windsor Great Park.

The Duchess discusses with television interviewer David Frost a book she helped edit, *The Palaces of Westminster*, by Sir Robert Cooke.

The royal couple share a joke before dinner at the Duke's Naval base in Dorset. It was their first public appearance after the announcement that the Duchess was expecting a baby.

The Duchess appears for a London film première in a controversial gown by French designer, Yves St. Laurent. Fashion critics could not decide whether the dress, which she also wore in Los Angeles, was magnificent or a jolly duvet.

United in grief. Grim-faced, the Princess and the Duchess arrive at RAF
Northolt following the skiing accident in Switzerland that killed their close
friend Major Hugh Lindsay.

"Exiles Night" when all the deposed or uncrowned heads of Europe who are in the direct line of succession to the British throne gather within the thick Castle walls. King Constantine of Greece, King Michael of Rumania, together with the Yugoslavian royal family, and Prince Philip's German cousins join in the festivities. While the usual routine is to troop around the castle on a glorified guided tour, these meetings do occasionally have a more serious purpose. One Christmas saw discreet soundings about the suitability of King Michael's daughter, Maria—now working as a secretary in Glasgow—as a possible bride for Prince Charles. This familiar evening ritual was given a new noisy life by Diana and Sarah. They turned the Waterloo Chamber into a disco, and with paintings of the generals who fought in the last Napoleonic battle looking down, they proceeded to dance the cancan, their long evening dresses swishing over the parquet floor.

This was but a rehearsal for their first public performance when the girls, accompanied by Prince Charles and the Duke, flew to Klosters in Switzerland for a week-long skiing holiday. (The Duchess had earlier spent a few days on the slopes with her friends, Peter and Clare Greenall—itself something of a novelty at Court. Royal Princesses rarely holiday alone.) The royal foursome lined up in front of the cameras near to the notorious Wang—the ski run where a year later Prince Charles's friend, Major Hugh Lindsay, was to lose his life so tragically. For sheer absurdity this annual spectacle takes some beating as ninety men and women of the press laden down with ladders and cameras scramble for positions in the fog, six thousand feet above an Alpine village. The Princess and the Duchess of York took this silliness at face value and staged a cabaret on ice where they indulged in mock conflict, pushing and shoving each other until Prince Charles announced censoriously, "Come on, come on!"

In public Diana's skittish humor has only been seen in rare flashes, invariably clouded by a mask of blushes and droopy silences. Her behavior when a group of royal photographers bumped into the royal party in a café in Klosters illustrated how her friend had revived her confidence. Instead of the expected awkward silence and glower, the Princess was all smiles, joking about the outsize medal on her jacket. "I have awarded it to myself for services to my country because no one else will," she said, laughing as Cockney photographer Arthur Edwards called her "luv" rather than "ma'am." If nothing else, the Duchess has taught the Princess the simple fact that the media have a job to do so she might as well get used to it.

The mood of frivolity in Klosters continued in the same vein. One night the girls enjoyed a brisk pillow fight in their secluded chalet at Wolfgang. On another evening as Charles, Andrew, and Sarah watched a video at the chalet, Diana dared to venture out to a local disco on her own. It was the Duchess's friends she met, dancing with Peter Greenall and chatting to merchant banker Philip Dunne, a friend from Sarah's childhood. This meeting between Dunne and the Princess—the first of several encounters—unfortunately provoked rumors about their relationship. Sadly Diana was made to pay a public price for her newfound independence.

It would be wrong to characterize the mood on that holiday as a glorified schoolgirl's outing. As one chalet guest recalled, "They all got on very well. It was good fun but within reason. You have to mind your p's and q's when royalty, particularly Prince Charles, is present. It is quite formal normally and can be rather a strain."

Indeed the added formality of Sarah's royal elevation has fundamentally altered the nature of her friendship with the Princess. They may appear to be equals at Court but some are more equal than others. The Duchess must forever pay discreet but formal obeisance to the Princess. It is a deference she is happy to concede to the friend who will one day be Queen. The social niceties between them are subtle, and the distinctions elusive—but they do exist.

What is more, they are sisters-in-law in an extremely competitive family. By nature the Windsors are achievers—Prince Philip and his internationally renowned carriage driving and the Princess Royal and her medal-winning horsemanship are but two examples. Rivalry in this royal family, as in royal families down the years, is second nature. It is for the most part good-natured, but there is no denying it exists.

Between the Duchess and the Princess that rivalry occurs not in the obvious fields of fashion or good works, but in their circle of friends. As Diana becomes more involved in Sarah's circle, there is a degree of competition as various friends ally themselves to one or another royal figure. Now that both are leaders of society, each one attracts groups of camp followers within their closed aristocratic circle. The talk for the time was of "NBFs"—New Best Friends—and of who was "in" and who was "out" in the regal roundabout.

Sarah's first Royal Ascot as a Duchess exposed all the underlying tensions between her and Diana of surface jollity and submerged anxiety. As they walked through the Royal Enclosure, the Princess prodded various friends, including Lulu Blacker, with her brolly. The Duchess, deferring to her friend, went along with the merriment.

As they continued from the Enclosure through the throng to the Paddock where the thoroughbred horses are displayed, the Princess noticed Princess Michael of Kent and wolf whistled. The Princess Michael turned and smiled in recognition. Finally, they arrived at the Turf Club, an unusual venue for royalty and a place usually avoided by established society. As the Princess made for a table at the back of the room she said in a stage whisper, "Let's get drunk." She proceeded to enjoy a glass of champagne ensuring that the party with her, mainly the Duchess's friends, missed the next race. As guests of the Queen, they were expected to see the race from the royal box. It is considered a discourtesy not to return. However, the Princess explained that she would smooth the matter over with the Queen. In the meantime the Duchess had returned to the royal box—as expected—and was disappointed to discover that her friends had stayed with the Princess and in so doing incurred the Queen's displeasure. Black mark for Fergie. The Princess never did apologize to the Queen, and the Duchess's friends were left feeling they had committed a social *faux pas*. As one friend said later, with some feeling, "The Princess feels that Fergie has stolen her thunder and taken the limelight. So she does silly things, and because Fergie feels that she has to support her friend she gets the blame. The Princess is very insecure and worries that people might forget her."

The watching world, not privy to the Courtly minuet, chorused its disapproval. "Far too much frivolity," sniffed the *Daily Express* as other commentators accused the girls of behaving like actresses in a soap opera. The criticism only served to draw them closer, if they bothered to read the sniping at all.

Tragedy was to draw them closer still. In March 1988 the Prince and Princess of Wales and the Duchess made their annual skiing pilgrimage to Klosters in Switzerland. After the obligatory photocall where Diana fell over in front of the cameras, the royal party went off to enjoy the slopes in peace. Under clear blue skies Prince Charles led five friends down the highly dangerous Wang run. As they neared the bottom the party was overtaken by an avalanche. The wall of snow killed the Queen's former equerry, Major Hugh Lindsay, and badly injured Charles's skiing friend, Patti Palmer-Tomkinson. Charles himself missed death by inches and was deeply shocked by the tragic affair.

That accident in Klosters was all the more poignant as both the Duchess and the Princess were friends of Major Lindsay's wife, Sarah. The couple had only been married for a short nine months, and Sarah was seven months pregnant when the accident happened. Sarah Lindsay, who works as a Buckingham Palace Press Officer, and the Duchess had struck up a particular friendship over the months, and when she too became pregnant in the New Year they enjoyed long lighthearted chats about the dubious delights of impending motherhood.

The Duchess herself could so nearly have been on that tragic run. Indeed, when a Swiss doctor arrived at the scene of the accident her first words were "Is it Fergie?" For once the gods were benign to this young woman who has the reputation of being accident prone. On that fateful morning as the royal ski party discussed their plans for the day over breakfast in their timbered chalet in the hamlet of Wolfgang, the omens did not look good. The Duchess, who had sailed through the early critical days of her pregnancy, was feeling distinctly queasy while Charles and Diana had a tiff about where to go.

She wanted to stick to the safe pisted runs, he wanted the challenge of off piste snow. The angry Princess dug in her edges and refused to ski with him, leaving the Duchess little alternative but to stay with her friend.

Until that moment she was in favor of skiing with Charles—morning sickness or not. The two girls skiied off together, the Duchess planning to join the "advanced" skiers that afternoon.

Once more the gods smiled on her although she didn't think so at the time. As she was coming down the black Christobel run she took an uncharacteristic tumble and landed ignominiously on her back in a mountain stream.

After hobbling back to the chalet a local doctor examined her and, bearing in mind that she was pregnant and had been warned by her own gynecologist Anthony Kenney not to ski excessively, decided to spend the afternoon resting rather than join Prince Charles on that tragic ski run.

The Duchess later told a close friend: "Klosters was a nightmare. I wish I had taken the advice to stay at home. I can't believe I was lucky enough not to have been skiing that afternoon."

In those harrowing hours following the accident, the royal friends comforted each other. Although eight hundred miles away in the Bay of Biscay, the Duke shared his wife's grief and sense of loss, a loss made keener several hours later when a Lynx helicopter from his ship, *HMS Engadine*, crashed into the sea killing its two crewmen. When the Duchess and the Princess arrived back at RAF Northolt to greet the grieving widow of Major Lindsay they looked simply what they were, two friends red-eyed with sorrow and tears who had been thrown even closer together by tragedy. Both displayed a dignity of bearing and a fellow feeling that made so much of the recent sniping at them seem churlish.

As the years shade away we will see a clearer light shed on their separate styles—the Princess of Wales as the distant icon, the perfect Madonna figure of the royal family, contrasting with the Duchess of York's warm ebullience and more humanly flawed public persona.

They will remain friends even though the nature of that bond will subtly change as they take on the burdens of monarchy. Already the Duchess has proved herself steadfast, loyal, and true, giving succor and support to her husband, her closest friend, and the royal family.

Like the Queen Mother she has the character and the underlying gravitas to become a firm bulwark against the hazards lurking in the decades to come. She knows her destiny. She is determined it will be fulfilled.

7

A People's Person

F *able, fantasy, and myth* have consistently formed a central role in the reality of the royal family. Once inside the charmed circle, the Duchess was herself sprinkled with the elusive stardust that makes dreams come true. The mere mention of her name can now fill large reception halls with smiling, eager faces and a royal word makes strong men reach for their wallets. She has exploited the mystique surrounding royalty to the full, acting as a businesslike fairy godmother to help raise millions of pounds for a clutch of charities. The most telling example of her style and breathtaking energy has been her work for the Search 88 Cancer Trust.

Gareth Pyne-James was a determined twenty-nine-year-old who gave up his marketing job with a steel company in South Africa to come to Britain to broaden his horizons and make his fortune. He arrived at Heathrow Airport with £1,000 in cash, no friends, and fewer contacts. Among his most precious possessions were treasured memories of a close friend, Valerie Stewart, who had tragically died of cancer. He wanted to do something to remember her name. The charity Search 88 was the result. It was based on the simple principle that if private sponsors would pay the charity's operating costs, all donations would be able to go directly toward cancer research and relief.

He outlined his ideas for the charity in a prospectus and then pulled the one string he had for all it was worth. A distant cousin of his girlfriend, Susan Tatham, knew Major Ferguson. Using his tenuous connection he arranged to meet him at the Guards Polo Club. His ambition was limited to asking the Major to stage a charity polo match on behalf of Search 88. Major Ferguson was impressed by his enthusiasm and commitment and agreed that he would put the Search 88 prospectus before his daughter. In the meantime, Gareth made presentations to captains of industry like Lord King of British Airways to try and encourage sponsors to fund the project.

Then came the breakthrough he had dreamt of. He received a letter from the Duchess's private secretary, Helen Hughes, summoning him to Buckingham Palace. The meeting was set for 11 A.M. on January 5, 1987. Gareth had been in the country a matter of months. He recalls, "I was so excited and nervous. My mother, Yvonne, flew over from South Africa to calm me down and to make sure, as she put it, that I washed behind my ears. Before I went to the Palace I got hold of a copy of *Debretts'* to find out how I should address the Duchess. As a foreigner I didn't know whether it was Your Royal Highness or Your Grace. The night before I spent ages practicing my bow in front of my girlfriend."

He arrived an hour early and spent the time marching up and down Buckingham Palace Road rehearsing what he would say. "I was very apprehensive," he remembers, "but once I was taken to her study the Duchess made me feel very welcome." In spite of the relaxed, friendly atmosphere his ideas came under close scrutiny. Where would the money go? Would Gareth benefit? How was the charity to be set up? The Duchess's questions were endless and incisive. She was delighted when he argued that black tie dinners were not part of his fund-raising formula. "Excellent," she said. "It's all very well putting on a ballgown and trotting out to a function but that only touches a small number of people. You have got to try and involve as many people as possible."

At the end of Gareth's forty-five-minute grilling they talked about their mutual love of flying before the Duchess dashed off for another appointment. As the Privy Purse door closed behind him and Gareth walked away from the Palace, his scheme could so easily have crash landed. Here was a smooth-talking young man with no track record or social contacts who had literally walked off the street and into the hallowed royal sanctum of Buckingham Palace. The Duchess would have been forgiven if she had listened to the voices of caution and politely declined the invitation to become the charity's patron. It was a gamble she was prepared to take, for here was the perfect opportunity for her to impress her own ideas on the world. The scheme attracted her precisely because it was fresh, involved the business world in a creative way, and had an egalitarian appeal. She insisted that she would not be a token figurehead but an active working patron.

While Gareth was setting up the charity's offices in Soho, he had the idea of producing a book in aid of Search 88 of photographs of Britain taken on a particular day and by ordinary members of the public. It was based on a similar highly successful project undertaken by a South African charity. Given her publishing background the Duchess was immediately enthusiastic. Moreover, the royal backing that her role as patron implied convinced a number of large companies to become involved, and soon the charity's staff were hard at work organizing this record-breaking event. The plan was to deliver Search 88 envelopes to every household in Britain asking them to take pictures for submission and to send in a donation to the charity. The Duchess was in daily contact and would supply her own ideas and comments. Her network of friends in business and society was ruthlessly exploited. A second meeting at Buckingham Palace was arranged in March, where the Search 88 team and the Duchess ran through the details of the proposed book, *One Day for Life*. Mock-ups of the book jacket and the leaflet were presented. She cast a professional eye over the designs, rejecting one as too gaudy, another as inappropriate, and selecting a picture of a sunset that was similar to the version of the finished book. She agreed to use her name and picture on the leaflet but insisted that the names of the sponsors were not nearby so that it would not seem as if she was endorsing their products. Gareth recalls, "The tone of the meetings was brisk and professional. She was full of practical suggestions and ideas. Had we thought of how to reach the people in the Orkneys? Had we got Terry Wogan to do something? Had we organized the media? That kind of thing." However, the Palace meetings were not entirely devoted to work. One cancer charity worker, Beverley Bailey, was ticked off by the Duchess for smoking forty cigarettes a day. "It will ruin your skin," she warned her, forgetting the fact that she herself had only given up smoking shortly before marrying Prince Andrew.

The fully fledged charity was launched in June 1987 at a reception for four hundred at the Dorchester Hotel. Shortly afterwards, Gareth Pyne-James came to fully appreciate the drawing power of a royal name and the commercial pressures that squeeze their preferred charities. He recalls, "Virtually every day a big company would phone me promising thousands of pounds if we could produce the Duchess at a business event. Many were household names who wanted to link the Duchess with their products to give them a better image. If it wasn't big business it was high society wanting to rent the Duchess. One lady from Dallas in Texas offered the charity one million dollars if the Duchess went to a society ball and opened a department store. On every occasion I refused. Otherwise we would have been in a 'Rent-a-Royal' situation where the charity was in effect being 'bribed' to produce the Duchess to the highest bidder." On the contrary, the aim of Search 88 was not to pander the élite but to involve the mass of the public.

August 14, 1987, was fixed as the date when people would

be asked to photograph an aspect of life in the British Isles. The response was extraordinary, with more than 110,000 entries pouring into a sorting office in High Wycombe, Buckinghamshire, where a team of volunteers and a panel of judges set to work sifting out photographs that best re- flected life on that day. Once again the royal name had drawn the stars into the project, and television personalities Terry Wogan and Selina Scott, together with comedian Kenny Everett and Olympic athlete Daley Thompson, all became involved.

When the Duchess joined the royal family for the annual holiday at Balmoral she insisted on being sent constant progress reports. It was not all good news. The organizers told her that they were facing difficulties sustaining media interest and the morale of the army of sorters required a boost. Typically, she agreed at short notice to visit the Buck- inghamshire sorting office to help keep the name of Search 88 in the news, demonstrating her awareness of the media when she presented her own entry, a blown-up picture of Crathie Church near Balmoral Castle, to a surprised Gareth Pyne-James.

During her time with the charity she had made a number of friends. One of the most special was Clive Jermain, a very brave young man who was confined to a wheelchair with spinal cancer. When he was seventeen he was told by special- ists that he had only a matter of months to live. At twenty- two he had written a highly acclaimed BBC play, *The Best Years of Your Life*, presented a television show for the disabled called "Open Air," and acted as spokesman for Search 88. A song called "Hold On," written about his suffering, was released to coincide with the launch of the charity. Sadly, even the Duchess's photograph on the cover failed to stop it from flopping in the charts. "Too morbid for breakfast listening" was the verdict. In spite of Clive's suffer- ing, the Duchess admired his cheerfulness and his ability to break free from the confines of his wheelchair and let his imagination roam. Sometimes he roamed too far afield. He got lost as he was being driven to meet the Duchess at the hastily arranged engagement in High Wycombe, and although the visit had officially ended, she waited for several minutes for him to arrive so that she could give him a token of her affection, an enamel pill box. A small gesture but typical of her royal style.

Several weeks before that meeting Clive had collapsed and been taken to the Royal Mardsen hospital in Fulham. Three times he was given the last rites, and three times he fought his way back from the clutches of death. Visits from celebrities and the knowledge that every day the Duchess was calling to check on his progress gave him the will to pull back from the brink.

Sadly, several months later he lost his unequal struggle. The Duchess sent his mother a handwritten note of condolence and a simple wreath of white freesias and tulips with a message that summed up the thoughts of many, "To a very courageous man, may you now rest in peace." Before he died, he and other Search 88 workers had shared the delight of seeing their book *One Day for Life* reach the number one slot on the bestsellers' list after being in the bookshops for just three days. Gareth Pyne-James phoned the Duchess at Buckingham Palace to tell her the good news. He recalls: "Her response was typical. It wasn't 'well done me' but congratulations to you all. Yet she had done so much to make it all a success."

Naturally the Duchess's pregnancy and birth of her first child meant that in 1988 her work for various charities including Search 88 was scaled down. Nevertheless, the pace was still fairly furious. Even after she had concluded a highly successful tour of California in March 1988 when she was fourteen weeks pregnant, she arranged a meeting with the Search 88 organizers just an hour after her twelve hour flight from Los Angeles was scheduled to arrive. In the event, her plane was delayed and the meeting was cancelled.

However, in the maelstrom of organizing and setting up the Search 88 charity, the Duchess was careful not to forget the true purpose of the scheme—to help cancer sufferers and aid research into the disease. She has made a number of private visits to hospices and the homes of cancer victims, as well as reading up on the medical background of the illness.

This pattern of private visits at grassroots level is echoed in other charities where she is patron. Her guiding principle has been to select organizations in which she is genuinely interested and then to work behind the scenes to see how they operate before undertaking public functions on their behalf. "I'm a people's person," the Duchess insists. It is her thoughtfulness and generosity of spirit that impressed the royal painter Michael Noakes during their nine hour-long "sittings" for her first-ever picture as a Duchess. "The Duchess is clearly anxious to use this remarkable influence she now has to the best possible advantage for deserving causes and she is aware of how helpful she can be to charities. The Duchess is a kindly person rather like Queen Elizabeth, the Queen Mother and she wants to use her office in a constructive way." She is now an active patron of thirteen charities ranging from drug dependency and care of the lonely to the Tate Gallery Foundation. They have come within her orbit thanks to a haphazard mix of friendship and good fortune. For example, a new charity called the Anastasia Trust, which aims to set up an international cultural center for the deaf in London, approached the Duchess simply because they liked the look of her face. The Trust's leading light, Lady Annaly, explained, "Her face is incredibly animated and mobile and if you are born deaf then the fact that she is so physically vivacious does communicate itself." The fact that the property developer Peter Palumbo is the Trust's chairman and also a good friend of Major Ferguson was a significant factor in convincing the Duchess to become president. "Her presence gives us tremendous street credibility," says Lady Annaly. "That is vital with a new charity."

Discreet lobbying by the Duchess's friends does indeed bring results. Her doctor, Michael Gormley, is closely involved with the Chemical Dependency Centre that acts as a counseling and halfway house service for those with drug-related problems. Dr. Gormley casually asked her if she would be interested in becoming involved, and to his surprise she was very enthusiastic.

The Duchess has seen the dangers of drug abuse firsthand for during her bachelor days, James Blandford, the Duke of Marlborough's drug-troubled heir, was a frequent guest at Paddy McNally's Verbier chalet. While Paddy had a strict house rule banning the use of drugs, everyone knew about "Gloomy" Blandford's heroin addiction. Sarah and other friends including Lulu Blacker had tried vainly to steer him away from that twilight world. One friend recalls, "They would spend hours convincing Gloomy that he would end up dead if he didn't get help. He would agree with their arguments and promise to do something. Then he would do completely the opposite. Just like addicts do." Blandford's tragic life made a profound impression on the Duchess, and when Dr. Gormley explained the work of the center in providing a drug-free environment for addicts, she was delighted to become a patron. She subsequently met Barbara Clark, the daughter of singer Petula Clark, who told her emphatically, "If halfway houses didn't exist, I don't know what I would have done."

She made an informal private visit to the Centre's headquarters in an unprepossessing church building in Fulham and met volunteers and architects who were converting two houses into halfway homes. Here she got a feel at first hand of the aims, ideals, and problems facing the charity that was set up in 1985 by Tristan Millington-Drake. He had seen his own father succumb to alcoholism and, after taking a training course in America, returned to Britain determined to help addicts.

As in her personal relationships, when the Duchess becomes involved with a charity she gives it her full support and thought and is invaluable in helping the credibility and reputation of relatively new charities like the Centre. On the evening of a ball in aid of the Centre an anonymous donor left £400 for the Duchess's charities in a bag at the side door of Buckingham Palace. She immediately handed it to Millington-Drake. She thought first of the Centre's needs once again when a Canadian businessman gave the Duchess $5,000 for a charity of her choice during her tour of the country.

When she attended a charity viewing of a four-minute film to illustrate the work of Sports Aid she was so impressed that she asked the producer, Andy Page, who is noted for television commercials about chocolate and men's deodorant, to do a similar show for Search 88. The result was a cinema film about the work of Search 88, filmed at the Royal Marsden Hospital in London and presented by the Duchess—the first member of the royal family to appear in a commercial.

The Duchess will often become involved in a charity for personal reasons. Her love of the art world and friendship with the Foundation's polo-playing former chairman, Peter Palumbo, encouraged her to agree to be made patron of the Tate Gallery Foundation. Her days in Clapham made her aware of the work of the Carr Gomm Society, a charity founded in 1965 and based in south London which provides housing for single lonely people. Again, she agreed to become patron of the Winchester Cathedral Trust because she had known and loved this magnificent cathedral from her Hampshire childhood. The path was smoothed by the fact that the chairman of the trust, the Lord-Lieutenant of Hampshire, Sir James Scott, is a friend of Major Ferguson. Indeed, the triumvirate of old school tie, aristocracy, and clergy still have a pervasive influence in the charity world. For example, she agreed to become president of Action Research for the Crippled Child because she knew a committee member through a friend. Since becoming president she has helped to raise £200,000 which has gone directly to help children suffering from water on the brain and hemophilia.

The magic exerted by the presence of royalty should not be sneered at. When the Duchess visited Cardiff on behalf of Action Research, the Fergie Effect was described by charity worker Caryl Jones: "Everyone was over the moon to be part of such a special day, and we were all impressed with the Duchess's natural enthusiasm and her detailed knowledge of the charity's work. Our excitement continued well into the night, with committee members telling me that they felt 'all tingly' to belong to Action Research for the Crippled Child."

While her network of old friends had involved her with some charities, in others, such as Search 88, the link has been quite fortuitous. One Sunday, Major Bill Anderson was sitting in front of his television watching David Frost's interview with the Duchess about her book, *The Palace of Westminster*. The Duchess spoke about the suffering of the author, Sir Robin Cooke, and his battle to finish the work while succumbing to motor neurone disease, an illness that attacks the nervous system. Major Anderson, who works for the Motor Neurone Disease Association, was so impressed that he contacted the actor Sir Anthony Quayle who is active in the charity and together they wrote a letter begging her to become patron. Almost by return post he received a letter agreeing from Helen Hughes, the Duchess's private secretary, who wrote, "Your letter in fact preempted a telephone call I was going to make to the MDNA to inquire whether there was anything her Royal Highness could do to help."

In her interview with David Frost the Duchess emphasized how her publishing job working for the Geneva-based entrepreneur, Richard Burton, meant so much to her. "The busier you are the more you get done," she explained. "It's a tonic, it keeps me in touch with the world around me, and it takes about twenty-five hours a day but I just make sure there's time. The girls in the office insist I'm a workaholic which drives them mad. And I want to do it because at the end of the day when Andrew comes back I have actually done something; I haven't just been sitting there wondering what I'm going to put on the next day."

From the start of her married life the Duchess set herself a punishing schedule, trying to dovetail her publishing job with her growing charity portfolio, particularly the Search 88 Cancer Trust, and her day-to-day royal engagements. The book which she had commissioned in 1983, *The Palace of Westminster*, took up much of her time. Even on her honeymoon she was reading and correcting proofs supplied by Sir

Robin Cooke. Toward the end the project became a race
against time as Sir Robin's condition deteriorated as the
disease spread. The Duchess's encouragement and the love of
the buildings where Sir Robin had served as a Member of
Parliament for Bristol gave him and his wife the will to carry
the project through.

The Duchess's determination to carry on working after her
marriage did raise a few eyebrows within the Palace. A
number of courtiers and several older members of the royal
family felt that the royal family was being drawn too close to
the commercial world, and that the Duchess herself would
not be able to do justice to both her royal role and her
publishing career. The Duchess argued strongly that her
work kept her in touch with the outside world and in this way
enabled her to perform her royal duties more effectively. "You
can combine the two as long as people understand just how
much work there is in both aspects of my life." "Anyway," she
says resolutely, "I like challenges!"

Her publishing work meant regular phone calls to Switzerland as liaison with printers, and lengthy working lunches
with her boss, Richard Burton, usually at Scott's, the fashionable Mayfair fish restaurant. She also used suites in various London hotels to meet Lady Cooke and the historian,
Penelope Hunting, to discuss the editing of the 431-page
volume. Her commitment included addressing a sales conference at Macmillans, who distributed the book and further
discussions with executives at Buckingham Palace. She even
helped to secure the inclusion of two stunning watercolors of
the Palace of Westminster that were originally presented to
Tsar Nicholas I when he visited London in 1844 and now
held by the Soviet authorities. The Speaker of the House of
Commons, Mr. Bernard Weatherill, mentioned the fact to
Mr. Gorbachev when he visited Westminster, and there then
followed an exchange of telegrams to organize their repro-
duction in the book.

It was a tricky balancing act and inevitably she lost her
footing as she tried to combine her publishing work, learning to fly, charity work, royal duties, and a controversially

large number of holidays to exotic countries. The crunch came when the book was published in November 1987 to a fanfare of publicity and a handful of television and radio interviews. By then the Duchess's honeymoon with the media was over. Her flippant boast that she worked twenty-five hours a day was cruelly caricatured. The *Today* newspaper led the charge in an editorial entitled: "Who are you kidding?" It fulminated, "The sooner she learns the difference between a day's work and a day's play the better." Other critics attacked the groveling style of television toward royalty and asked why the Duchess had been interviewed in the first place. One complained, "When Penelope Lively won the Booker prize were we subjected to her commissioning editor waffling on about long hours, too much work?" Even within the royal family there was concern that she had used her royal position to gain commercial advantage and profit for her company. "A mistake," one member of the family felt, "I don't think the royal family's name should be used in this way." Unfortunately, the Duchess became the whipping girl for a general mood of disgruntlement about the behavior of the royal family, particularly its younger brethren. Normally, the public are in favor of royalty and do not begrudge them their riches provided they behave responsibly and do not flaunt their privileges. As the Queen Mother once advised her daughters, Princess Elizabeth and Princess Margaret, "Your work is the rent you pay for the room you occupy on earth."

It is the Queen Mother who is largely responsible for creating the present acceptable royal image of a family of simple people, dedicated, unsophisticated, shunning fast fashionable society, and making little attempt to fraternize with even the most low-brow intellectual. This respectably suburban image is one of the reasons why Princess Michael of Kent, with her exquisite good taste, rich Arabian friends, and enjoyment of high art, finds few admirers among the general public. She has to live with a royal tradition where King George V thought "high brow" was spelled "eye brow" and where the present Queen's father, George VI, threw a book at a royal courtier for daring to suggest he should patronize the opera more frequently. It explains why the Duchess found herself so out of favor for pursuing her publishing work. She did not conform to the stereotype of the demurely dutiful Princess and, with her free holidays in the sun and the snow and her free flying lessons, seemed to be leading a hedonistic, dilettante lifestyle where work took second place to pleasure. The charges do not stand up to close scrutiny but in the looking glass world of royal life, image is reality. It was something of an own goal, especially as the Duchess had to stand comparison with the Princess Royal who worked tirelessly for the Save the Children Fund in some of the most desolate parts of the globe. Yet just a few weeks after the publicity surrounding the book, she was to close that particular chapter in her life and end her five-year association with Richard Burton.

She had already shown her publisher around the Royal Library at Windsor Castle where they discussed plans to catalogue and reproduce George III's collection of Italian architectural drawings. "Ideal weekend work," Burton joked about the five-year project. However, neither had anticipated the ferocity of the stock market crash and the collapse of the American dollar.

Just weeks after the Duchess had so enthusiastically spoken about future projects in her television interview with David Frost—"I'm going to keep on going, it's in my blood now," she had insisted—Burton flew over to London from Geneva to discuss with her the implications of the financial climate for his business. He had decided to close down his Geneva company and open a new venture in California investing his energy in a revolutionary electronic method of reproducing Old Masters. The news came as a blow to the Duchess and as a victory for those inside the Palace who were dubious about her business aspirations.

Burton maintained a diplomatic silence, and the news that his publishing company, BCK Graphics, had gone bankrupt only leaked out after the Duchess's pregnancy had been announced. Fortuitously, the impending birth and increased royal work load would have inevitably curtailed her publishing work. However, she is determined to remain in publishing, working on a freelance basis and undertaking projects as and when she has the time. Many will no doubt be in the field of charity publishing, an ideal combination of the demands of royal protocol and her own interests.

In the established arena of traditional royal engagements, the ribbon cutting, the glad-handing, and the pleasant small talk, the Duchess has demonstrated her own magic qualities. Indeed, on her first public outing following her honeymoon she proved such an irresistible draw that two young punk runaways returned to a special school in Sunderland just to see her. Her contribution to the royal roadshow has been significant even though she is still something of an apprentice. In the year of her marriage she made forty-six royal visits—only twelve behind her husband and in 1987, her first full royal year, she performed 132 public duties in Britain and spent thirty-six days abroad flying the Union Jack. "She has got off to a flying start," says Tim O'Donovan, the compiler of the royal Wisden. Some estimate of her value for each appearance came when television personality Selina Scott was paid £3,000 for stepping into her royal shoes when the Duchess had to cancel an engagement.

Unlike the Princess of Wales, the Duchess needed only a little coaching before she was confident and competent enough to cope on her own. She has undertaken a bewildering kaleidoscope of royal engagements, from walkabouts along the cobbled streets of York, to opening a babycare ward in a Cardiff hospital to planting trees in Putney, and viewing the work of sculptor Henry Moore in a city church. Many of her duties have involved her charities, others have been the inevitable society round of balls, first nights, and gala banquets in aid of worthy causes. One minute dressed in a sensible two-piece suit, the next dressed up like the fairy on a Christmas tree. When she wishes to dazzle she can always borrow a tiara or diamond broach from the Queen's collection at Buckingham Palace. She has ridden the thoroughbred racer Aldaniti along the Long Drive at Windsor Castle in aid of cancer charity and exchanged her jodhpurs and hacking jacket for Yves St. Laurent originals for a gala night.

The girl who was once to be seen continually in the same skirt and baggy wraparound has come to realize that life as an actress on the royal stage means many costume changes. In the early days at Buckingham Palace she had so many expensive Manolo Blahnik shoes that the corridors outside her rooms, with the portraits of the Duke of Windsor, Queen Mary, and George V staring down, were used to store them. If she paid the full price for her wardrobe of Devoriks, Ronays, MacKinnons, Blairs, Chanel, and St. Laurent, she would have little change out of a million dollars. She does get them at cut-price, for it helps when your mother-in-law is the richest woman in the world. Even so she moans to friends about the size of her overdraft.

The Duchess is a natural at that vital element of royal stagecraft, the art of small talk. Chatting to complete strangers in the rain on a walkabout or enjoying a verbal fencing with comics like Dudley Moore and artist David Hockney is her stock in trade. Only rarely is she overawed, as when she behaved like a star-struck fan on meeting singer David Bowie. She is the quintessential public relations girl, never lost for an answer or a quick retort.

The journalists who trawl in her wake, like so many sea-gulls following a mackerel smack, find that she throws few scraps in the way of off-beat or personal remarks to whet their appetites. She may reveal that she enjoyed watching Morecambe and Wise when she lived at home, or that she stayed up late to catch Crown Green bowling on the television, and she loves arranging her own flowers—freesias and roses are her favorites. Normally she sticks to the royal script of "How are you?," "Have you been waiting long?" and "How long have you been a scout/nurse/pensioner/sea lion?" Unlike the Princess of Wales, who will occasionally come out with odd impromptu one-liners—"I'm as thick as a plank" is one of the more notable unscripted efforts—the Duchess is still happy to be the obedient understudy. But she has her moments. She managed to bring a blush to the cheeks of Bible-thumping Chief Constable James Anderston when she accused him of wolf whistling at her during a visit to a Manchester hospital. Her style is chatty, exuberant, watchful, and physical. She and Andrew are a knockabout royal double act—frequent slaps on the back, goggle eyes, and pointed fingers leave observers in no doubt that she is in command of the performance. While she worries about protocol it does not stop her from taking pictures for spectators or slowing down the schedule because she is having a good chat. She has a memory for faces and an appreciation of people. The Duchess does take time and trouble, like when she picked out pensioner Mike Wager during a visit to the Royal Chelsea Hospital because he had served with three generations of her family in the Life Guards.

Rather like the Prime Minister Margaret Thatcher, she has a bustling schoolmarmish manner with the same unfortunately waddling walk. She sails into crowds, seemingly supremely confident, sometimes overconfident. Her friends know better. When she tries too hard to please they see her compensating for her basic shyness and disguising her nerves. "Yes," said one of her closest friends. "Fergie was very shy as a schoolgirl. It was Paddy McNally who brought her out of herself and I think she will always be grateful to him for that." Yet her friendliness is now sneered at as "flashy" by the very same newspapers and pundits who once praised her for knocking the stuffing out of the royal family. She frets about her performances and cares about the people she meets.

It was a typically spontaneous gesture when she bought young Martin Hartley, who lost all his family in the Zeebrugge ferry disaster, a toy truck which he so desperately wanted. She had it sent to his home in Derbyshire by special messenger. She shows concern and compassion for life's victims, a caring exhibited during her visit to the injured in hospital in Belgium. As one commentator put it, "The Duchess has yet to acquire the sort of film star adulation of the Princess of Wales. Thus she was able to discharge her duties without the uncomfortable spectacle of the public gawking to see what she was wearing and to ask the questions we might ask, offering the same sympathy we would offer." This is the key to adulation surrounding the royal family. They are an elusive combination of Everyman and Superman. The Duchess is now part of the fable that is the House of Windsor. Her flaw is that she will not veil herself in the Garboesque mystique so brilliantly achieved by the Princess of Wales.

The pressure is there for her to make that subtle change from commoner to royal, to place an undefinable distance between herself and the masses, to be cool, aloof, and distant—a princess on a pedestal. She will never be that. She is a friendly, outgoing girl, someone who is not afraid to live at street level. Her openness and her transparent eagerness mean that she does not fit easily into a predictable role within the royal repertoire. She is not a fairytale princess. Her character is that of the people's princess, the girl who rewrote the royal script and brought a little life and laughter to a somewhat starchy royal revue.

8

The New Yorker

The Duchess of York pulled desperately on her wooden paddle, shards of freezing spray whipping into her face and soaking her green combat trousers. Her sixteen-foot canoe bucked and plunged in the angry, white foaming torrent as she strained to keep the craft afloat. Behind her Arctic expert David Thompson bellowed instructions, his voice snatched away amidst the roaring of the rapids. As the water banked up endlessly around their frail Mad River kayak, Thompson searched frantically for a clearer stretch, using all his sixteen years' experience of the notorious Caribou Rapids to try to navigate their craft to safety. He knew that if they capsized in these icy waters they could survive for just seven minutes, no more. His heart and head pounding with exertion, he struck out with his heavy wooden paddle, guiding the boat through the surging waters. Like the proverbial cork from a bottle they popped out of the narrow gorge and as the Hanbury river widened they both slumped over their paddles, their faces flushed from their furious attempt to escape the clutches of the remorseless rapids. For a long minute they were silent as they caught their breath, their paddles trailing in the smoother waters. Both realized how close they had been to capsizing in the freezing river. Then the Duchess turned around to David and said with a grin on her face, "Well, that certainly got the heart pounding." They laughed and paddled to catch up with Andrew and the other five members of their party.

David, a lean and fit Toronto lawyer, recalls those frantic few minutes where they fought the river and almost lost. "The Caribou Rapids are a very long stretch of rough water. For a time there didn't seem to be too much of them. But halfway down, the water just piled up and piled up. If you didn't know what you were doing you would have had it, that's for certain."

Fortunately, during the planning for the two-week canoe trip at the end of their Canadian tour in 1987, they had decided to team up with David, a highly experienced wilderness guide, with the Duchess, a novice with a canoe. The decision proved vital as they paddled through the rapids. David remembers, "The Duchess immediately realized that it was very dangerous. I shouted instructions, and she did exactly what was ordered. My heart was going, I can tell you. This had been my nightmare before the trip—how to explain to Buckingham Palace that you are bringing back one less person and a Duchess at that. You are a long way from any help in the wilderness. You can't afford to take any chances and going through those rapids our luck nearly ran out."

It was the most nerve-racking few minutes on the ten-day trip, a holiday that was the climax to a highly successful first tour of Canada by the Duchess. In her two-year royal career she has criss-crossed the globe, flying the flag for Britain. Her pioneering spirit struck a chord with the North Americans who warmed to her eager style and openness. Those same qualities of enthusiasm and informality have been attacked at home for showing too much of the common touch. The commentators who like royal princesses to be like porcelain have discovered that the Duchess is beyond the ornamental, disregarding the constraints of expected royal decorum.

Besides Canada, her other major visits have been to California, New York, and a projected six-week tour of Australia, together with shorter tours to Mauritius, France, the Netherlands, and Jersey in the Channel Islands. But it was her tour of Canada in July 1987—her first major foreign visit— that showed the Duchess in private and in public, giving a vivid portrait of her style and personality.

The mood was set from the start. When the Canadian authorities sent a long memo to Buckingham Palace asking about the likes and dislikes of the royal couple, the reply was short, sharp, and startling, "No food preferences, no allergies, they will do anything within reason." As one Canadian official said, "They are the only members of the Royal Family ever to have put no restrictions on their itinerary." However, by the time they visited Los Angeles six months later the Duchess, then expecting her first baby, was more careful. She requested no melon or avocado on the royal menu and after six days of bland official banqueting food told one aide, "I'm dying for a cheeseburger."

While the Duchess was game for anything, she was understandably apprehensive before embarking on her first major foreign tour, a visit which meant much to Andrew who had spent two terms at Lakefield College in Ontario and grown to love the people and the scenery.

By their very highly scripted nature, royal tours yield few genuine news stories for the media army who follow the royal trail. It means that there is an inordinate amount of attention paid to fashion. As one Canadian journalist perceptively noted, "Unless we're the party faithful invited to chat with the Royals, we're relegated to hanging around doorways and lining up in gutters. And, sadly, the clothes are our only real point of contact."

As she prepared for the trip the Duchess had a real problem. She had a "terrifying overdraft" and the dress allowance from the Foreign Office which controls royal tours, amounted to a meagre £2,000. Her lady-in-waiting, Helen Hughes, was entitled to the princely sum of £750 to pay for her changes of clothing during the twelve-day visit. Unlike the Princess of Wales, the Duchess does not have a private income to draw on—Prince Charles earns £1 million a year from the Duchy of Cornwall—and the Queen is reluctant to pay the bills for public duties out of her private purse. In the weeks before their tour she bartered and bargained with a number of fashion designers, including Edina Ronay and Zandra Rhodes, to put together a fitting wardrobe. Normally a day's itinerary required three separate changes of clothing—some forty different outfits for the tour.

It meant that she carefully chose the big events to show off new dresses, packing her old outfits for the run-of-the-mill engagements. She even rented a Klondyke gown from a local fancy dress company when she appeared at the Wild West Fort in Edmonton, Alberta. As one friend who helped organize her wardrobe admitted, "The Duchess wanted to make a big impression on the Canadians. She wanted to do well for Andrew but she was terribly worried that the fashion people would unfairly compare her with the Princess of Wales and pull her apart."

She realized that fashion was often the only way the female members of the royal family could communicate with the public, and she was fearful that the Canadians would gain the wrong impression of her. So it was with daring that she walked down the steps of the royal jet at Toronto wearing a jolly red maple leaf—the national emblem of Canada—in her hair. It was a deliberate compliment to her hosts and showed a willingness to take a chance at the expense of her royal dignity. These hair decorations have now become a regular feature of her tours. In Los Angeles she had two hair pins with the letters "L" and "A" in the back, and on another occasion she had the Union Jack and the Stars and Stripes flags as patriotic fashion emblems. "Check out the hair, boys," she told photographers as she wore the flags, a comment which some saw as a sign of brashness. "It's really nerves," explain friends. "The photographers are familiar faces so she talks to them, blurting out the first thing that comes to mind."

Her tours, particularly in North America, have displayed her frivolous approach to fashion. It is fashion as fun, as theater. Her friend Marina Killenary, who made a hat for her with two birds nesting in a bed of roses, explains, "Straight, high fashion styles bore the Duchess to death. She prefers quirky, fun fashions." Once again, the Duchess shows a similarity to the Queen Mother in her early royal life, both using their clothes as props, seeing royal tours as long-running theatrical events.

The point is perhaps best made by comparing them with their contemporary "rivals," the Princess of Wales and the Duchess of Windsor. Wallis Simpson always exuded a sense of studied style, a cool chic which many found too sophisticated. How one wonders would her tailored precision have coped with visits to the bombed out East End of London during the Blitz? The Princess of Wales is noted as an international fashion plate with an unerring ability to hit the right note. The Queen Mother and the Duchess of York, however, are frivolous fashion leaders, where clothes are reflections of their vivid personalities.

In her day the Queen Mother, as Duchess of York, faced acid comments about her extravagant styles. When Wallis Simpson was asked how best the Duchess of York could promote British fashion abroad, she replied scornfully, "Stay at home." Yet, as Sir Cecil Beaton said of her, "She has all the unreality of a spangled fairy doll on top of a Christmas tree. The effect she creates is dazzling." Where would we be without the sight of the Queen Mother in her floating blue or green chiffon, outdated platform shoes and flowery hats? They are as familiar as close friends and as reassuring as the monarchy itself.

As the Queen Mother heard of the criticisms of the Duchess's effervescent manner she will no doubt have recalled the horrified reactions to her first tour of New Zealand and Australia in 1927 where she plunged into crowds, shaking hands, and chatting, unheard of before in sober Court circles.

When the present Duchess visited Canada and California her hosts were delighted because here too was a royal lady who actually spoke. During a trip to Washington made by the Princess of Wales, Americans were bewildered by the fact that it was Prince Charles who did all the talking, even when questions were aimed at his wife.

The Duchess is no silent statue with a "Fragile, handle with care" sign around her neck. The only fragile part of her is her hands. Like Prince Charles's they tend to swell and become sore with too much hand-shaking. As a precaution she invariably wears white gloves. Her hands are ever mobile as she works the crowds, pointing, gesticulating, waving over Andrew, punching him on the shoulder and patting him on the bottom. During a walkabout in the center of Toronto she delighted the crowds by holding onto the balloons she was offered, standing on a concrete sleeper so those at the back could get a better look and then play-acting a dive into an ornamental pond. And when, during a flight to Niagara Falls, their Huey helicopter had to make an emergency landing in a field she joked, "What else are we going to do today for excitement?"

Larry Kent, the Ontario media coordinator, was impressed by her style—"She plays the crowd very skillfully, as though she has been doing it all her life. She is concerned about those in the back row as well as the front. It doesn't sound much but for those waiting for hours under a hot sun it means the difference between a day made and a day spoiled."

During that visit to Niagara Falls she picked out a little girl, Erin Marazzo—a victim of cystic fibrosis—and accepted a flower she had picked from her garden. The Duchess had noticed that she was near to tears because her view was being obscured by the crush of the crowd. As one Canadian commentator noted: "In so many ways this royal couple seem just like us. And yet, with just the acceptance of a flower and a few kind words they have the power to lift the spirits of a dying child. But that's the magic of royalty."

The Duchess's thoughtfulness was demonstrated when she

used a trailer caravan, loaned by a local couple, to act as a changing room before she practiced her canoeing on the river at Minden in northern Ontario. While she was changing she spotted a guest book in the corner of the trailer, opened it and signed her thanks for their hospitality. "They were just ecstatic," recalls Larry Kent. He considers her the best member of the royal family since the Queen Mother in her attitude to the media, "It is almost as though she has been taking lessons from her, she is so aware of the camera positions."

While Buckingham Palace officials on the tour tried to limit media access to the royal couple, the Duchess often overruled their decisions, a sign of her increasing confidence. As they cruised on the *Maid of the Mist* beneath Niagara Falls, the Duchess ordered Andrew on deck so that the media boat, which she had authorized against the wishes of her aides, could take pictures of them.

Time and again she demonstrated that she was not the passive partner in her marriage. "Where is Andrew? Is he all right?" she asked anxiously on numerous walkabouts and public events. The electricity between them fires and crackles almost constantly.

John Latimer, the royal visit coordinator, who was with the royal couple throughout their visit to Ontario was captivated by their togetherness. He recalls, "They were extremely warm, caring, and a lot of fun. There was a lot of banter back and forth, but they both knew that she was the star of the show."

Andrew said as much when he admitted that wherever they went he was always sitting on the "wrong" side of the car. "It's Sarah they want to see not me," he said, reminiscent of the Prince and Princess of Wales's visit in 1983. It was also Sarah they wanted to hear. She was greeted with tumultuous applause when she grabbed the microphone from him during a banquet in Edmonton. She playfully gripped him by the throat for his earlier remarks about her and then proceeded to make an impromptu speech boisterously thanking the Canadians for their hospitality.

Again, as previously discussed, when she made a speech to

an audience of celebrities and politicians in Los Angeles, a Democratic senator, Art Torres, overcome with chablis and bonhomie, shouted "I love you" as she reached the lectern. The Duchess paused, looked in his direction and said with a twinkle in her eye, "I will see you later." While the remark brought the house down, it renewed accusations that the Duchess was being overfamiliar, a criticism guests at the banquet firmly refute. One British consulate official admitted, "The man was an embarrassment throughout the evening and her riposte struck just the right note. It managed to shut him up."

Her willingness to take a risk by being upfront was shown when she and the Duke accepted a pair of fur coats from the governor of Alberta. They were told about the surprise gift just an hour or so before the presentation in Edmonton. It was a classic dilemma—to refuse the coats would have offended their hosts, while to accept would anger animal rights campaigners. The Duchess was not only delighted to be given the fur but insisted on trying it on in front of the large crowd. Since then she has worn the fur, a symbol of Alberta's trading past, when she has gone skiing in Switzerland. The irony is that the fur itself was imported from South America.

Fur is one thing, snakes quite another. While the Duchess is a country girl who rides and takes her Labrador dog for daily walks, she has a genuine phobia about snakes. She burst into tears in public when a twelve-foot python was held before her at the end of a charity polo match in Connecticut. This fear was seen two months earlier when the couple took two days break from their Canadian tour to waterski and canoe by Lake Muskoka. At the end of their stay they emerged from their wooden cabin for a group photograph taken with the sixty members of the Ontario Tactical and Rescue Unit—equivalent of the SWAT squads—who had guarded them. Larry Kent recalls, "All the men were standing up ready to have their pictures taken when the Duchess let out a piercing shriek and jumped about two feet in the air.

Then she screamed for Andrew to come. There in the road was a very dead snake. It was so dead there were tire marks on it. Andrew just laughed when he saw it, but she cowered away and wouldn't go near the thing."

She also developed a rapid aversion to a certain type of tree, the *homo sapiens*, during that stay by the lake. As they relaxed, twenty-five policemen had literally gone undercover, taking hours to camouflage themselves as shrubs or small trees. They had stayed in the woods around the clock watching for potential intruders. When the Duchess came over to thank the squad for their efforts it was the first time she had really noticed them.

"You lot look like trees," she joked.

"Ma'am, we are trees," was the rather wooden response.

"Where were you guys?" she asked, rooted to the spot.

"In the woods round the house," replied the walking tree.

She called for Andrew. As he came wandering over, she told him that they had been protected by these "trees."

"We were planted everywhere," said the tree when the Duchess quizzed him further. She went bright red knowing that she and her husband had been unwittingly observed in private at this romantic spot by a branch of the security forces.

On their first wedding anniversary—July 3—they held a private party in Edmonton for tour staff, where Andrew gave Sarah a gold pin decorated with a heart and a bee—and a celebration kiss. That evening the Duke and Duchess were able to behave like an ordinary married couple, dancing and laughing among friends. As one official recalls, "They were extremely natural, having fun and behaving like two young kids in love. At one point he teased her, throwing bread-crumbs in her direction and she chased after him with a glass of water in her hand. They were just horsing around."

The physical side of their relationship is tempered by a caring concern for each other's welfare, a feature noted by David Thompson during their arduous canoeing trek. "They are very much in love," he observed. "The Duke was always looking out for her to make sure she was OK. For example, when we portaged he would always be on hand to give her help with her pack and the canoe. He is very careful of her, very watchful, very loving."

Portage, a term describing the rigors of carting sixteen-foot long kayaks and fifty-six pound packs over rocky countryside when the river is too rough, was just one of the dubious pleasures of that trip. The Duchess had never canoed before and was deeply apprehensive about her ability to complete the journey. Her nerves showed at the photocall held on a fly-blown beach beside Sifton Lake, deep in the Canadian barrenlands. "I don't think I can stand ten days of this," she moaned as she manfully heaved her pack over her shoulders, letting out a great "Cor blimey" yell when the weight settled. "I've got no hairdryer," she added good-naturedly as she wafted away the clouds of biting black flies. Indeed, for the first five days the flies drove them wild, in spite of wearing nets and smothering themselves in copious quantities of the deterrent musk oil. At night she was bothered by the noise as the bugs battered the tent. She was just as worried about putting her dubious culinary skills to the test, but she had to muck in with the rest, one day on the roster for the washing up, another for the cooking. David recalls with a chuckle, "Her cooking has improved but there is room for further improvement. We forced her to cook and she did manage to make a strawberry shortcake which was quite edible."

Their days started at seven in the morning, when the sun was already high in the Arctic sky. After a cooked breakfast, they broke camp and paddled on down river taking a ten-minute break every two hours. Lunch was usually jam and bread with cheese, nuts, and salami, washed down with a flask of water. They did a little fishing for trout and pike, some trekking to ancient Indian sites, and an awful lot of portage. "What have I let myself in for?" the Duchess groaned regularly. They had a quick swim at the end of the day but the water was too cold for anything as daring as skinny-dipping. The group talked about the wildlife—they saw peregrine falcons, caribou, but no grizzlies—the weather, their families, and for once the Canadians managed to turn the tables on the Duchess.

On the first night a few of the party, which included Andrew's former headmaster Terry Guest and his wife and old schoolmate Don Grant, went into the tundra saying that they were going to collect ptarmigan eggs. It was a ritual that would have to be performed each night if the party wanted fresh eggs. David recalls, "We disappeared over the hill, yelled and screamed, ran around the tundra flailing our paddles. We then painted and rolled in the dirt half a dozen Grade A large eggs we had brought with us." When they showed their finds to the Duchess they told her that she would have to find fresh ones the next night. She was puzzled, wondering how on earth such a small bird laid such large highly colored eggs. "Finally, the penny dropped, but for a while she was very worried she was going to fail us," says David.

As they got to know each other better David became more impressed by the Duchess's qualities and her benign effect on Andrew. He recalls, "She has an unbounded enthusiasm for life, is interested in pursuing as many things as she can, and is fascinated by the lives of other people. I remember one day the weather was rotten, it was cold and miserable, and I thought it would have got her down. 'Aren't you fed up?' I asked her. She said, 'No, this is lovely. It reminds me of Balmoral.' If that is northern Scotland then save me from it. That is her—a very positive attitude to life and very competitive in a friendly way with Andrew. Marriage has certainly matured him. He is very much more aware of the people around him, aware of his sense of responsibility, and eager to be a fully fledged member of the team."

The royal couple left their Canadian friends with comments about babies ringing in their ears. David recalls, "We talked about another canoeing trip and joked that by the time that was organized they would have lots of children running around them. It was they who said 'No way' and clearly outlined their intentions to remain childless for some time."

Five months later the Duchess discovered she was expecting her first child—but nothing would stop her from fulfilling her foreign engagements. However, unexpectedly the mood of the public and press in that short space of time had changed towards her. What was once admired as fun, was now defined as frivolous, youthful exuberance was now seen as undignified immaturity. The shift in attitudes was a combination of the behavior at Ascot of the Duchess and the Princess of Wales, the controversy surrounding the Royal Knockout Tournament, and a general feeling that Sarah was enjoying too many holidays in the sun. Just as Princess Margaret riled the public in the 1950s and 1960s by jetting off in the middle of the British winter to the Caribbean, so the Duchess angered many by her freewheeling, cosmopolitan lifestyle. A streak of puritanism in the English national character feels the royal family should pay for its privileges in the currency of duty. The Duchess, it was felt, was not giving value for money. It was a view not helped when, after spending a few days at an exclusive hotel in Mauritius following their week-long official visit, the Yorks's scheduled jumbo jet destined for Paris, flew first to London especially to drop them off. Their fellow passengers were not amused and neither were the British public.

When the Duchess flew on the Concorde to New York to be the guest of honor for the opening night of Andrew Lloyd Webber's hit musical, *Phantom of the Opera*, there were a few grumbles but no more. Most concern surrounded an incident where an IRA supporter lunged at the Duchess as she was returning to her Broadway hotel.

Greater criticism was voiced when she and Andrew flew to Los Angeles for a ten-day tour in late February 1988 to support British arts in that city. It was perhaps appropriate that it was in Hollywood—land of dreams and fairy tales—that the Duchess's love affair with the British public hit its first major row. Lionized in Los Angeles, in London the Duchess was like a lamb to the slaughter. Her choice of fashions, her off-the-cuff comments, and her boisterous behavior with Andrew, racing him across a manicured lawn on golf carts, all added up to the question: "Has the Duchess of York gone too far?"

Ironically, most of her dresses which attracted so much adverse comment had been seen before in Britain. "Why get new ones when they won't fit me for long?" she had sensibly said. Yet an Yves St. Laurent gown, described as "dazzling" at a London film première, was variously ridiculed as a "duvet" or a pair of old curtains. Hollywood fashion designer Richard Blackwell attacked her for looking like "a common chambermaid" who "walks like a duck with a bad leg." In Britain more than one commentator remarked that their "cringe-making immature antics" were bringing the monarchy into disrepute, citing the occasion when she broke a fake glass bottle over her equerry's head during a tour of a film studio. A similar act by the Princess of Wales upon Charles's crown earned the photographer who captured the image a top award.

Nevertheless, when the British journalists covering the tour returned home they were bewildered by the vitriol which had been poured over the Duchess's head by pundits whose opinions were formed less by the facts of the tour and more by circumstantial evidence of the last few months. Ingrid Seward, editor of *Majesty* magazine, noted, "I was surprised at the bad publicity at home because the Americans thought she was terrific. They admired her pioneer spirit and the fact that she was so informal."

The actor Michael York, who was a member of the UK/LA festival committee, said, "Britain should be proud of the sterling services performed by two of the most attractive members of the royal family. Their schedule was hectic and covered a great deal of ground. People were astonished at the royal couple's vitality and delighted by their dignity and charm." In the city itself the views and a number of local dignitaries inspired the *Los Angeles Times* to comment, "Now Los Angeles has put up its dukes, in protection of a young couple it has clearly adopted, received, and perceived as Crown Jewels." Yet critics argue that the Duchess of York is a commoner who is seen as being too common, a young woman who overstates her enthusiasm and energy.

It is worth pausing to remember that other members of the royal family can and do come unstuck when they are abroad. Prince Philip managed to put his feet well and truly in it during the Queen's historic tour of China with his infamous comment about "slitty eyes." When the Princess Royal, who now has a public image as the royal equivalent to Mother Theresa of Calcutta, visited Washington several years ago, Americans were so disappointed in her miserable demeanor that one commentator sputtered, "Why not limit Princess Anne to opening rhododendron shows in Kent before unleashing her again on foreigners?" And it is only a few short years ago that Prince Andrew's paint-spraying tour of California was dubbed on television "the worst royal visit since they burnt the White House in 1812."

The Duchess of York will continue to tread her own path through the perils of public opinion. While commentators may try to criticize her, she has proved to be a superb ambassador for Britain, generating enormous goodwill and affection on each of her overseas visits. She has become a highly visible "invisible export" for the country and a genuine credit to the royal family.

9
Dynasty

*I*t *could have been so different.* A quiet life as a naval wife in the decent obscurity of a Services base. Occasional outings in the glare of the public spotlight but only when family duty called. Like the Princess Royal's husband, Captain Mark Phillips, the Duchess of York could have been content with continuing her career and enjoying the peace and privacy of a comfortable family life as she watched her daughter, Princess Beatrice Elizabeth Mary of York, grow and develop.

Instead, historians will look back on 1988 as the year when the Yorks's family dynasty really began to take shape. The birth of a princess, who is fifth in line to the throne and the first princess born within the royal family since Princess Anne in 1950, together with a new home under way that is the first example of royal building in this reign gave ample indication of the way ahead.

It is all entirely in character for a young woman who runs when she could walk, and works when she could rest. She relishes motherhood in the same way that she has coped with the challenges of the first thousand days. "She will make a marvelous mother," says her father, Major Ferguson, without a trace of bias. "She is kind, caring, she loves children and they love her." Her stepmother, Susan, is equally enthusiastic. "She always gives children a good time, she's forever romping with mine. But she is a disciplinarian who likes to see children well behaved."

However, children are but an element, albeit an important one, in a rich and diverse marriage. "She's not the sort of person to sit at home doing nothing, far from it," says her father. Typically, during a pregnancy that was traumatic and emotionally stressful, she found time to write two children's stories about a helicopter called Budgie—the nickname she gave to the flying machine she trained in.

As her closest friend and former flatmate Carolyn Cotterell remarks, "Sarah is a very organized person and such a capable girl she will find it very easy to fit her baby into her busy life." The Duchess symbolized her wish that she should not be cosseted and pampered on the afternoon of Monday, January 25, 1988—the day Buckingham Palace officially announced her pregnancy. The Duchess drove to RAF Benson and went for an eighty-minute flight in Budgie, her Jet Ranger helicopter. She flew over Dummer, where her stepmother Susan held out a sheet with the misspelled message: "Congrats Ma'm." Everyone was delighted at the news, even the gossip queens of Fleet Street. Jean Rook of the *Daily Express* gushed, "This sensible, good-humored, warmhearted and open-minded mother-to-be will make a mark on her child's life more valuable than any royal crest."

The Duchess was determined that pregnancy would not affect her hectic schedule—at least not in the early months. She enjoyed a skiing holiday with friends at the Swiss resort of Klosters and made a lightning quick stop in London before flying to New York for a charity gala on Broadway. No sooner had she arrived back at Buckingham Palace than she was packing her bags again, this time to Meribel, in France, as patron of the Combined Services Winter Sports Association to watch a skiing competition.

While doctors warned her to take it easy, the Duchess continued to ski. "I'm a hundred percent fit and I always moderate my skiing to suit the condition," she said jauntily. However, she was aware of the miscarriages suffered by both her mother and sister Jane, yet had complete confidence in the medical judgment of her Harley Street gynecologist, Mr. Anthony Kenney. She runs her life on common sense, not cotton wool, and her diagnosis was that she was fit and able to carry on active life well into the late stages of her pregnancy.

Traditionally, royal ladies have been treated by the Court gynecologist, Mr. George Pinker, who has delivered all the royal babies over the last decade. However, in the past the Duchess had seen Mr. Kenney, a consultant at the private, American-owned Portland hospital, and decided to stay loyal to him.

While there was much talk about her irresponsibility in skiing when pregnant, few noticed that Mr. Kenney accompanied her on her Los Angeles tour and that she had a second ultrasound scan before leaving as a further safety measure. Indeed, displaying the anxiety of many first-time mothers she even requested amniocentesis to assure her that the baby was healthy. However, as this procedure carries with it some risk of miscarriage, Mr. Kenny sensibly advised against it.

For the first critical few weeks, all was well. Unlike the Princess of Wales, she managed to avoid the agonies of morning sickness, although her complexion, normally free of blemishes, did suffer. However, as her royal friend did, she developed cravings for certain foods. While Diana lived on a diet of bacon and tomatoes during her pregnancy, Sarah developed what she termed a "fetish" for boiled eggs, toast "soldiers," and mayonnaise.

In the later months the Duchess suffered physically and emotionally. Her weight rose to such an extent that the bookmakers William Hill gave very short odds on her giving birth to twins.

She complained of feeling continuously sick and told friends: "I can't wait to get this whole thing over with." Her discomfiture was evident and the sensitivity she always had about her appearance was apparent when she visited an agricultural show in Yorkshire. When a young schoolboy offered her a rosette for a winning breed of Shire horse, she said, with evident feeling, "Who gets the rosette—me or the horse? I'm beginning to feel like a horse."

In spite of the problems, the Duchess was fortunate to secure the services of a nanny who was not only superb with children but an expert in karate—should photographers become too intrusive. Guitar-playing Alison Wardley, from Manchester, traveled to Buckingham Palace to meet the royal couple after being recommended by the Princess Christian College, where she had been the only pupil ever to win a distinction in the final exams. The Yorks, equally impressed by her sense of fun, her no-nonsense approach, and her calm patience, immediately recruited her as a £5,000-a-year nanny. Wardley says emphatically, "I'm a firm nanny but I'm not a battle ax. Children need love and security but they also need a framework behind them."

In the difficult last few weeks of the Duchess's pregnancy, when the weight and the waiting became endlessly tedious (even the Queen said that she was "fed up" with all the waiting), she had no husband by her side to comfort her. The Duke was transferred from his base at Portland, Dorset, where he had been a weapons training instructor to become officer of the watch on board the frigate *HMS Edinburgh*. He joined the ship in May where he teamed up with an old Navy friend, and now his commander, Captain Alastair Ross. The frigate set sail in mid-June for a three-month voyage to Australia as part of the Outback 88 task force which arrived in time for the naval celebrations to commemorate the country's bicentennial.

Just days before he left, he was on hand to comfort the Duchess when her father, Major Ronald Ferguson, was featured on the front pages of several Sunday tabloid newspapers with details of his secret visits to a massage parlor in London's West End. She was distraught by the unsavory publicity and the subsequent effect on her family, particularly her loyal stepmother, Susan Ferguson. Naturally, the experience gave her a more jaundiced view of the media. She remained loyal to her father, giving him moral support at the height of the scandal, when there were calls for him to resign from the post of Prince Charles's polo manager.

There was even talk that the Queen had asked her to distance herself from her father, arguing that the Duchess must show that her duty to the royal family, and hence the nation, came above her natural concerns for her own family. The Duchess was put in an impossible position and one in which she starkly realized the true burden of life in Britain's First Family: a life where love and affection comes a poor second to obedience and responsibility, where a harsh and remorseless reality lies behind the superficial gloss and glamor of the royal round.

The Duchess was paying a very heavy price for involving her family in her royal life. Indeed it is a feature of the Duchess's generous style that from the first she was determined that her family should join in the fun and not spend their days on the outside looking in.

Normally, the royal in-laws very rapidly become out-laws and the House of Windsor is happy to speed the process along. During a royal courtship Buckingham Palace gives the beleaguered families no help or guidance, and after the official announcement is made the portcullis clangs down. Earl Spencer, for example, was reduced to standing outside the Palace gates on the day that his daughter's engagement to Prince Charles was announced. As one friend states, not without some truth, "It seems to be a Havoverian trait to take over the girls who marry into the Family. Why couldn't Lady Diana have got married from Spencer House in London with the Spencer coach?"

The Fergusons could have followed the familiar pattern of a brief flare of glory and then relegation to the obscurity of the shires. But that hasn't happened, and Major Ferguson became an internationally known media personality, much as it may have irritated the stuffier members of society who sneer at him as a "social-climbing stable boy in a fancy blazer." While Major Ferguson is careful to call his son-in-law, "Sir," it now surprises no one that when the Yorks attend official functions the Ferguson clan occasionally come along as well. The Duchess even took her grandmother, The Honorable Doreen Wright, with her when she went to see the ballet *Swan Lake* in Bath.

The galloping Major's own enjoyment of the spotlight meant that when he fell, he fell very hard. "Why did they pick on me?" he asked friends plaintively. The answer, sadly, is that fame exacts a fee in the corresponding loss of privacy. Those who court the limelight do so at their peril. In an ignominious end to a painful year, the Major found himself ousted as deputy chairman of the Guards polo club. The club committee, which voted unanimously, cited his financial acumen rather than his private exploits as the overriding reason.

The gods did indeed seem to be toying with the Duchess of York. In just a few short months, she watched her father humbled and humiliated; experienced the anguish of the Klosters tragedy, lost her publishing job; saw her favorite charity, Search 88, run out of sponsors; and, finally, just a few days before the birth, she was involved in a crash on the M4 motorway.

As the massed ranks of the world's media gathered outside the £350-a-night Portland hospital, there were lurid stories that the Duchess was suffering from toxemia and that she faced an emergency cesarean section because her baby was in the breech position. Characteristically, she faced these tales and setbacks with good humor, secure in the knowledge that the Duke would be by her side in the second week of August—the expected birth date.

A day after he arrived home from Singapore, the Duke and Duchess drove up to the back entrance of the eighty-six bed Portland hospital. For once the Nikon choir of photographers failed to serenade her. She handed her jolly gynecologist Anthony Kenney a bunny badge for luck as she settled in to her pretty third-floor room.

With the Duke and her mother, Susie Barrantes, hovering in the wings, Mr. Kenney decided to induce the birth rather than let nature take its course. Once labor started, around teatime, it was swift, vigorous, and very painful. The Duchess requested and was given an epidural injection to ease the pain of the four-hour labor while Andrew played the traditional role of concerned husband, holding her hand, mopping her brow, and whispering words of encouragement.

"She had a tough time of it, but she came through very well," he said, with some relief.

At 8:18 P.M. on the eighth day of the eighth month of the eighty-eighth year of the century, the Duchess's six-pound, twelve-ounce baby daughter came in to the world—a timing, according to the superstitious Chinese, of awesome good fortune. Another whim of the gods perhaps?

The traditional notice—typed by the Duchess's private secretary, Helen Hughes—was attached to the gates of Buckingham Palace just seventy minutes later. The three-line announcement, bearing the royal crest, read simply: "Her Royal Highness the Duchess of York was safely delivered of a daughter at 8:18 today. Her Royal Highness and her child are both well." It was signed by the medical team of Sir John Batton, physician to the Queen; Mr. Anthony Kenney, the Duchess's gynecologist; Mr. Barry Lewis, her pediatrician; Miss Tessa Hunt, the anesthetist and the Yorks's family doctor, Dr. Michael Gormley.

Both grandmothers were naturally delighted. The Queen, on board the royal yacht *Britannia* off the Scottish coast, hoped that her fifth grandchild would have curly hair, while Mrs. Barrantes was enchanted by the baby's "beautiful elegant hands."

The Duke was equally enthusiastic as he chatted to well-wishers, including pensioner Edith Bowdidge who had waited twenty-six days outside the hospital: "My daughter is gorgeous, but I'm biased. She is very pretty. It feels wonderful to be a father."

Family well-wishers, including Princess Diana and her two boys, Princes William and Harry, had a chance to see the new arrival for themselves.

While the Duchess enjoyed the splendid sight of seventy-seven rare red orchids that her husband had had flown specially from Singapore, the astrologers consulted their charts to plot the destiny of this eminently lucky Leo. The royal baby, they opined, would be "extroverted, confident, dignified—and marry a foreign king."

It soon became apparent that the royal couple had not decided on a name for their daughter whom they temporarily christened "baby Yorklet." While the souvenir industry held its breath, the Duke and Duchess continued their ruminations when the royal couple and their new Yorker left the hospital just four days later and flew north to join the Queen at Balmoral.

While the public made Annabel, Elizabeth, and Charlotte favorites, the royal couple eventually picked Beatrice, an eminently Victorian name that conjures up images of aspidistras, Gilbert and Sullivan, lavender, and old lace. It was a name chosen after hours of deliberation by the royal family, the Queen enthusiastic in her suggestions. They were not amused when the announcement of the name was prematurely leaked in a national newspaper. But the Queen was sanguine. "Let's remember that today's paper is tomorrow's fish and chip wrapping," she advised the irritated parents.

The last Princess Beatrice was Queen Victoria's youngest daughter and constant companion in her later years. As the Queen's eyesight began to fade, dutiful Beatrice would read out the secret government reports and memos. However, she rarely concentrated on this important task, much to the annoyance of the Queen's private secretary, Ponsonby.

At the time, Ponsonby wrote about Beatrice to his mother in vexed terms. "The Queen is not even au courant with the ordinary topics of the present day. Imagine Princess Beatrice trying to explain . . . our policy in the East. I may write out long precis of such things but they are often not read to Her Majesty as Princess Beatrice is in a hurry to develop a photograph or wants to paint a flower for a bazaar. Apart from the hideous mistakes that occur . . . there is a danger of the Queen's letting go almost entirely the control of things which should be kept under the immediate supervision of the sovereign."

The shy princess was also entrusted with the sensitive task of editing Queen Victoria's famous diaries. Here she behaved like a latter-day Oliver North, burning any material she deemed unbecoming before agreeing to the diaries' release in 1927.

This quiet, withdrawn young woman was also cursed with the royal disease—hemophilia—which she passed on to her three children. Indeed she led something of an ill-fated life. As a teenager she was profoundly affected by an incident when a maniac shot at her mother while they were both riding in an open carriage. Her dutiful husband, Prince Henry of Battenburg, who was Lord Mountbatten's uncle, died of fever after the Battle of Ashanti in 1896 (the same campaign in which the Duchess of York's great uncle, Major Victor Ferguson, died). And Princess Beatrice's daughter, Princess Victoria Eugenie—the grandmother of the present King of Spain—was nearly assassinated on her wedding day when anarchists threw a bomb at her coach. The old princess outlived all her brothers and sisters and when she died in 1944 at age eighty-seven, the famous society diarist Chips Channon noted: "Death, who has been on holiday recently, has just bagged old Princess Beatrice."

While the choice of Beatrice was greeted with mixed feelings by the public, her middle names of Elizabeth and Mary conformed to popular wishes. Elizabeth was an obvious compliment to the previous Duchess of York and Mary, her mother's middle name, maintained the Ferguson influence.

The couple's choice of godparents proved less of a problem than the choice of name and it met with public approval. The Duchess's influence was paramount. Her former flatmate, Carolyn Cotterell, her old schoolfriend and skiing partner, Gabrielle Greenall, together with the millionaire property developer Peter Palumbo, a close friend of Major Ferguson, were the godparents from her side; while the Duke asked

Viscount Linley, his cousin, and the Duchess of Roxburghe, the aristocratic friend who had proved so supportive during their romance.

Before he rejoined his ship, the Duke ensured that the whole event was very much a family affair by taking the first official portraits of his wife and daughter in the sitting room at Balmoral.

It was a short-lived family idyll. Once more the iron laws of royal duty prevailed as the Duchess decided to leave her six-week-old infant in the care of her nanny while she flew to Australia to undertake a ten-day tour of Canberra, Sydney, and Queensland with her husband. The Duchess did have the pleasure of a fleeting reunion with her sister Jane as she toured the Outback and kept in touch with the development of "Baby Beetroot" (her nickname for the infant) by having videos of her flown out to Australia in the diplomatic bag.

It was not enough, not nearly enough, for the public. They were dismayed that baby Bea was left behind, and this disappointment turned to anger when it was discovered that the Duchess planned to stay on in Australia for nearly a month to follow the Duke's frigate around the coast. In the resulting hysteria it was largely forgotten that the Queen, when she was Princess Elizabeth, had left two-month-old Princess Anne in the care of a nanny while she journeyed to Malta to join the Duke of Edinburgh. He was enjoying his first and, so it was to prove, his only naval command, HMS *Magpie*, and the couple spent several idyllic weeks together in the Mediterranean. The royal couple, married now for more than forty years, still look back on those days as some of the happiest of their lives. Certainly Princess Anne does not seem to have suffered.

However, those observations were brushed aside as the Duchess was labeled a "national disgrace" and a "terrible mother." Naturally the Duchess felt an aggrieved sense of persecution, knowing as she did that her husband was scheduled to be assigned to a sea posting until at least 1998. The castigation was all the more cruel given the care and consideration she had shown—especially to physically and mentally handicapped youngsters—during her official tour. Sadly, all her efforts and enthusiasm were overshadowed by the debate surrounding Princess Beatrice.

Indeed the soap opera quality of the entire trip—it rapidly developed into a kind of "Palace Dallas Down Under"—was underscored when it was revealed that the Duchess's sister, Jane, had left her Australian husband, Alex Makim, and that their eleven-year-old marriage had hit the outback dust. It was a further emotional trauma for the Duchess, who had suffered so much during an eventful and turbulent year.

While she juggles with the special problems of her long-distance marriage and the upbringing of her baby, the Duchess has not abandoned her ultimate aims of truly making a mark on the House of Windsor.

The construction of the Yorks's new home—the most important royal house to be built this century—is another statement of the Duchess's commitment to lead her life her way, to plan her own royal route and not simply follow in the well-worn path of those who have gone before. The cost of the house, estimated at £1 million, will be met by the Queen. It is her wedding present to the couple in the same way that she bought Gatcombe Park for the Princess Royal. The eight-and-a-half-acre site on the edge of Windsor Great Park no doubt inspired poignant memories for the Queen. She was given the plot by her father, George VI, as an engagement present. Unfortunately, the house that was there, an unpretentious eighteenth-century building embellished by James Wyatt, was destroyed by fire in August 1947, just months before Princess Elizabeth married and could move into it.

In spite of the obvious royal connections, the decision to build the Yorks's new home on protected land courted controversy. First of all, the sixteen-bedroom mansion set in rolling parkland contravened planning regulations, as it was sited in a conservation Green Belt zone at Sunninghill Park, near Ascot. While the country council rejected the plans for a two-story ranch-style building, the local Bracknell council was happy to welcome the Yorks with open arms.

Although the locals were generally pleased with their new neighbors, they were less content when several families living nearby—all workers on the royal estate—were asked to leave their homes. They were considered potential security risks because they were too near the proposed development. Local publican Mick Gillings complained, "I don't see why everybody should be disrupted just because they carry the badge of VIP."

The overall design of the red-brick gabled home—which has a nursery wing and staff quarters as well as tennis courts and a swimming pool—also attracted criticism. It was variously described as "Palace Dallas," "Southfork," and an army barracks. While the house, with its stables, courtyard, and grand entrance hall, did give the impression of a Texan ranch or a Tennessee mansion, the architect, Sir James Dunbar-Nasmith, commended the light and airy style and the friendly design. The Duke and Duchess regularly flew to his architectural practice in Edinburgh, Scotland, to see how the plans were progressing and to add their own observations and suggestions. Sir James, a leading exponent of building conservation and Professor of Architecture at Edinburgh's Heriot-Watt University, made his name by designing two Scottish theaters, although he first came to the attention of the Yorks when he did some work for the Queen at Balmoral.

It will take eighteen months to design the royal home but considerably longer to decorate the interior. For the moment, King Hussein of Jordan, a confidant of the Queen, has loaned the Yorks his English home of Castlewood House, which is conveniently near the royal building site. Even though she is a temporary resident, the Duchess has given the place a regal feel with silver-framed photographs of the family and cutlery engraved "E R" borrowed from the Queen.

Guests are shown plans by the Duchess, eager to explain the latest development in her new home. American visitors are particularly impressed, both by the style of the exterior and the names of the first-choice interior design consultants, the New York–based firm of Sister Parish and Albert Hadley.

The Duchess has firm ideas and she was impressed by the work of these long-established East Coast designers when she visited the home of her polo-playing friend, Henryk de Kwiatowski, during a stay in Connecticut. Encouraged by de Kwiatowski, who has had four of his six homes decorated by Hadley-Parish, the Duchess phoned the prestigious designers. "I'm sitting here in this wonderful chair . . . " she told the firm, pausing to add, "We're only number two so we don't have much money."

Her impulsive gesture of bringing in a New York interior designer once more provoked an outcry. "It is as if the royal yacht *Britannia* had been sent to Korea for a refit," fumed the *Daily Express*. For once the Queen, who was expected to pick up the estimated £1 million bill, interceded. She felt that the cost of decoration was a trifle high—even though the Queen is the wealthiest woman in the world. The Duke and Duchess were asked to think again and to consider the merits of British designers for this unique example of royal building.

Ironically, their choice was essentially the English version of Parish Hadley. They asked Nina Campbell, a designer known as the darling of the Sloane Set, to decorate their home. Her trademark is a feminine English look created through dainty prints on chintz, cotton, and linen.

Miss Campbell, described by her staff as a "strict perfectionist," met the couple at Buckingham Palace shortly before the birth of Princess Beatrice. She impressed them by her belief that a home should be cozy and comfortable. "People must be able to relax in a room," she argues. "You have to keep in mind that children will be coming in and out and that people have muddy shoes. It is essential that friends, children—and even your dogs—feel at home."

The Duchess agrees with that sentiment. Her home will be a hive of industry with various bee motifs—the emblem of her coat of arms—buzzing through the nursery and other rooms in the guise of wallpaper, carpets, and even solid-silver ashtrays. There will be a place too for the buffalo head the Yorks were given during their Canadian trip, for the signed photograph from the Red Arrows display team, and the numerous cartoons that currently decorate the Duke's study at Buckingham Palace. The Duchess has already enlisted the help of art dealer William Drummond to buy quirky little drawings and watercolors that might take her fancy.

The overall look will be Nina Campbell's responsibility— if the Duchess can afford her bills. Her style is casual, cozy splendor—sofas dusted with the hairs of the Duchess's pet dog, Bendicks, the pruning shears dropped on the desk, the never-too-new-feel for furniture. Ms. Campbell, who has worked for rock singer Rod Stewart and billionaire Adnan Khashoggi, has already begun work on the designs and fabrics for the Yorks' home. Her brief is simple. "The Duchess has made it clear it must be warm and inviting. A typical English country family home."

At heart the Duchess is a young woman who does the unconventional for traditional reasons. The flying, the canoeing, the new home have all excited comment but she has done them for her husband, her family, and for self-fulfillment. She has the dynamism and outlook of the New Woman, but her beliefs and values are worthily old-fashioned. Duty, responsibility, and hard work walk hand-in-hand with her independence, easy laughter, and sense of adventure. Royal life has merely served to increase her natural appetite for life. "Quite simply she is one of the smiliest, bubbliest people I've met," says her friend the designer Philippa MacKinnon.

The Duchess's effervescent personality has been firmly bolstered by two years of marriage, and her natural good humor has buoyed her through the transition from commoner to leading royal figure. Yet she still wounds easily. She cries in private because she cares about her public. Pleasing people was her way of life long before she joined the royal family.

Since then she has shown that she sincerely believes in the traditions, the mystique, and the magic of the fairy tale that is monarchy. Now that she has become part of that story, she is determined to tell it her way.

PHOTO CREDITS

The author would especially like to thank Major Ronald Ferguson for allowing us to reproduce the photographs from his family album: opposite p. 24 (top right and bottom) and p. 5 (top) of photo insert between pp. 24–25. We also thank Ritva Risu of Finland for the following pictures from her private collection: opposite p. 24 (top left); pp. 2–3 of photo insert between pp. 24–25, left (3) and right (top left and top right).

Thanks also go to the following sources:

Alpha: p. 7 (top) of photo insert between pp. 24–25

Camera Press Ltd (Portrait study by HRH Prince Andrew): p. 4 of photo insert between pp. 56–57

Mauro Carrero: p. 7 of photo insert between pp. 24–25 (bottom)

Lionel Cherruault: p. 4 of photo insert between pp. 120–21 (2)

Tim Graham: p. 4 of photo insert between pp. 24–25 (top)

Mail Newspapers plc: opp. p. 120; p. 7 of photo insert between pp. 120–21

Desmond O'Neill: p. 4 of photo insert between pp. 24–25 (bottom)

Photographers International: p. 5 of photo insert between pp. 24–25 (bottom); p. 2 of photo insert between pp. 120–21

Press Association Photos: p. 5 of photo insert between pp. 120–21 (2); p. 6 of photo insert between pp. 120–21

Rex Features: p. 3 of photo insert between pp. 24–25 (bottom); opp. p. 57; p. 3 of photo insert between pp. 120–21; opp. p. 121

Frank Spooner Pictures (Photo Julian Parker): p. 5 of photo insert between pp. 56–57

Syndication International: p. 6 of photo insert between pp. 24–25; opp. p. 25; opp. p. 56 (2); pp. 2–3 of photo insert between pp. 56–57; p. 6 of photo insert between pp. 56–57; p. 7 of photo insert between pp. 56–57 (2)

Index